Nonfiction Writing

Grade **2**

D1316325

Writing: Camille Liscinsky
Content Editing: Robin Kelly
Leslie Sorg
James Spears
Andrea Weiss
Copy Editing: Carrie Gwynne
Art Direction: Cheryl Puckett
Cover Design: Liliana Potigian
Illustration: John Aardema
Design/Production: Carolina Caird
Susan Lovell

EMC 6012

Evan-Moor®
EDUCATIONAL PUBLISHERS
Helping Children Learn since 1979

Congratulations on your purchase of some of the finest teaching materials in the world.

Correlated to State Standards

For information about other Evan-Moor products, call 1-800-777-4362, fax 1-800-777-4332, or visit our Web site, www.evan-moor.com. Entire contents © 2011 EVAN-MOOR CORP. 18 Lower Ragsdale Drive, Monterey, CA 93940-5746. Printed in USA.

Visit *teaching-standards.com* to view a correlation of this book's activities to your state's standards. This is a free service.

CPSIA: Printed by McNaughton & Gunn, Saline, MI USA. [6/2011]

Contents

Basics of Nonfiction Writing

Expository Writing

Nonfiction Writing • EMC 6012 • © Evan-Moor Corp.

Persuasive Writing

Narrative Writing

How to Use This Book

Nonfiction Writing provides 18 units of instruction and practice activities. Each unit focuses on a basic element or specific form of nonfiction writing and includes guided lessons and accompanying student pages. Each lesson targets a skill essential to that element or form. The units are grouped into four sections: basics of nonfiction writing, expository writing, persuasive writing, and narrative writing.

Teacher Pages

Use the lesson plans to provide guided instruction and modeling of the targeted skills in each unit.

A brief definition of the form offers a quick overview and simple wording to share with students.

Some lessons include an optional extension activity to further explore the skill or writing form.

The first lesson in each unit introduces key characteristics of the form and provides an opportunity to discuss and analyze a strong writing model.

Reduced student pages provide answers and sample responses at a glance.

The review lesson at the end of each unit guides students through the process of critiquing and revising a weak example of the writing form.

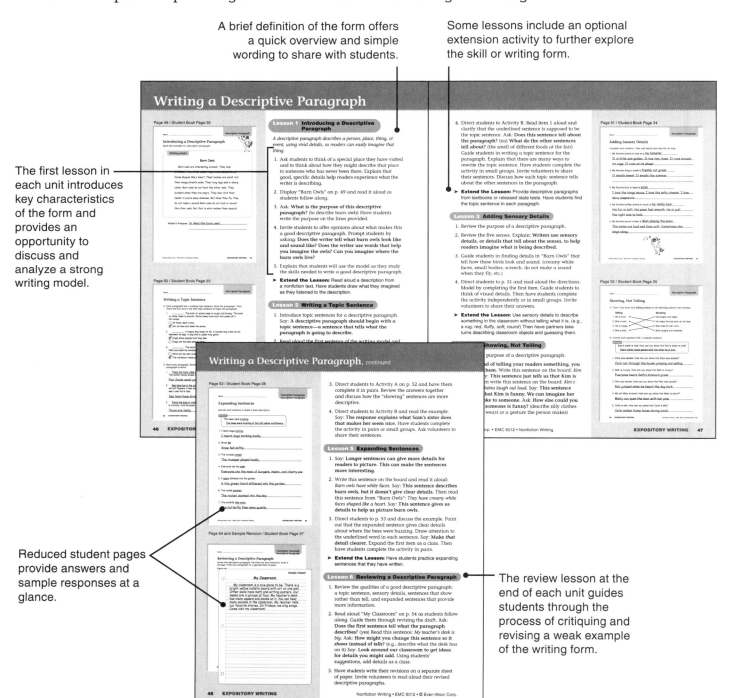

In each unit, students apply the skills they are learning by analyzing a writing model and completing a variety of focused activity pages.

Writing Model

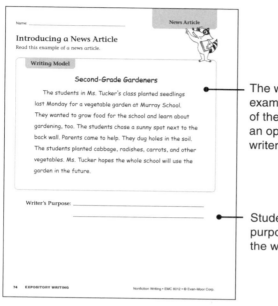

The writing model contains examples of key elements of the form and provides an opportunity to study the writer's craft.

Students connect the purpose for writing with the writing form.

Activity Pages

Students practice skills in a variety of activity formats designed to deepen students' understanding of the form and craft.

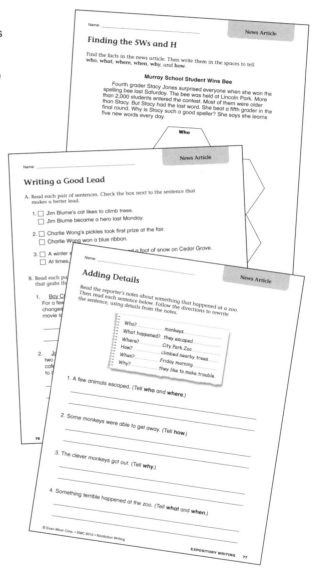

Review

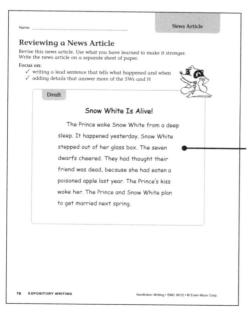

At the end of the unit, a weak model of the writing form is provided for students to revise, giving them the opportunity to review and apply all the skills they have learned.

Additional Student Pages

Three units in this book have unique pages that are necessary to provide the appropriate modeling and support for the writing form.

Response to Literature

The first and last lessons of the *Response to Literature* unit begin with a reading selection to give students practice analyzing a writing prompt and responding to it—just as they would on a test or homework assignment.

Introducing a Response to Literature
Read this fairy tale.

Reading Selection

Oscar and the Three Otters

There once was a family of three otters—Papa Otter, Mama Otter, and Baby Otter. One day, the family left home to go diving deep into the sea for tasty crabs. But the otters forgot to lock their door.

Oscar Octopus knew that the otters were away. So he crept right into their home. Oscar saw three crabs on the table. He took a bite of the biggest crab and spit it out. It was too chewy. Oscar tried the middle-sized crab, but it was too salty. The littlest crab tasted just right, so Oscar ate it all up. Then he saw three beds made from seaweed. The seaweed in one bed was too long. His arms got twisted up in it. The seaweed in another bed was too thick. It felt lumpy. The last bed was just right. Oscar crawled in and fell asleep.

Soon, the three otters came home. They saw bits of crab on the floor. Baby's crab was gone, and Papa's seaweed was in knots. Baby Otter yelled and pointed to the octopus asleep in the seaweed. Oscar woke up. He darted away in a cloud of ink. He did not even say that he was sorry.

Prompt: Is Oscar Octopus rude? Give three reasons why you think this. Use details from the story.

Introducing a Response to Literature
Read this example of a response to literature.

Writing Model

In "Oscar and the Three Otters," Oscar Octopus is rude to the otters. First, he goes into their home when he knows they are away. Second, he eats their crab and messes up their seaweed. Third, he leaves without telling the otters that he is sorry. Oscar Octopus is very rude.

Writer's Purpose: _____

Reviewing a Response to Literature
Revise this response to literature. Use what you have learned to make it stronger. Write your response on a separate sheet of paper.
Focus on:
✓ understanding the prompt
✓ writing a topic sentence that answers the prompt and names the story
✓ finding story details that help you answer the prompt
✓ using the story details in your answer

Draft

... The mice are different. First, he sleeps ... traw in a barn. Second, he gathers ... ds to eat. A cat chases the mice, so ... ntry Mouse wants to go back to the ... ntry. This is a good story.

Reviewing a Response to Literature
Read this fable about two mice.

Reading Selection

City Mouse and Country Mouse

One sunny spring day, City Mouse went to visit his cousin in the country. Country Mouse made a bed of straw in the barn. "You can sleep here, next to me," he told City Mouse. Then Country Mouse gathered seeds. "I've saved the best seeds for you," he told his cousin.

City Mouse stared at the straw. His whiskers twitched when he saw the seeds. "How can you eat such plain food? And how can you sleep in such a rough bed? Come to the city with me. I'll show you how to live."

So the two cousins headed for the city. The sun was setting when they reached the house where City Mouse lived. They pushed through a hole between the bricks to get inside. City Mouse fluffed up a soft cotton cloth. "This is where we will sleep," he said. "But first we'll feast!"

City Mouse led his cousin into the dining room. Bits of cheese, cake, and bread were all over the floor. The mice nibbled until they heard a hiss. "It's the cat!" shouted City Mouse. "Follow me!"

The mice ran through a small hole in the wall. City Mouse laughed and asked, "Wasn't that fun?"

"Not to me!" Country Mouse's heart pounded. "When that cat goes to sleep, I'm leaving. It's better to eat seeds and feel safe than to eat cake and be scared."

Prompt: How are the two mice different? Tell three ways. Use details from the story.

Summary

The first and last lessons of the *Summary* unit begin with a reading selection for students to summarize.

Introducing a Summary
Read this example of a summary.

Writing Model

"Snails and Slime" tells h... Snails use slime to move ar... stick to things. It keeps a s... sharp objects. Slime also ke... its shell in winter. Slime is g...

Writer's Purpose: _____

Introducing a Summary
Read this article about snails.

Reading Selection

Snails and Slime

A snail has a soft body and no legs. This means it is hard for a snail to move around. So a snail makes a layer of slime under its body. Slime is very important to snails.

Slime makes it easier for snails to move from place to place. It is strong and sticky. Slime helps snails stick to leaves or walls.

Slime keeps a snail from getting hurt as it moves. It lets a snail move across rough stones. Slime even lets a snail move across sharp glass without getting hurt.

Slime also keeps snails safe during winter. A snail can pull its body into its shell to stay warm. It covers the shell's opening with slime. The slime turns hard and keeps out the cold air.

People may think slime is yucky. But for snails, slime is great!

Reviewing a Summary
Revise this summary. Use what you have learned to make it stronger. Write your summary on a separate sheet of paper.
Focus on:
✓ writing a topic sentence that tells what the article is
✓ retelling ideas from the article in your own words
✓ putting the details in order
✓ writing a good ending

Draft

"You Can't Find Me!" tells how an... stays safe from sharks and eels. An... hides by making itself look like a pil... or sand. It can also hide in small pla... octopus uses ink to stay safe.

Reviewing a Summary
Read this article about an octopus.

Reading Selection

You Can't Find Me!

An octopus might look like a blob with eight arms. But this sea animal is a yummy treat for sharks and eels. So an octopus must use many tricks to hide and stay safe.

An octopus hides by making itself look like a pile of rocks or sand. An octopus can change its skin color to brown, black, gray, or orange. It also can make its skin look bumpy like a rock. Or it can make its skin look smooth like fine sand. It is hard for sharks and eels to find a hiding octopus.

An octopus uses ink to stay safe. If a shark or an eel comes too close, the octopus squirts ink. The ink makes the water dark, so the shark or eel cannot see. Then the octopus swims away.

Small spaces are good hiding places for an octopus. The animal's body is soft, so it can push itself between rocks or into little holes. Sharks and eels are too big to follow the octopus.

The octopus is a clever animal! It can keep itself safe from enemies that are much bigger.

Forms of Nonfiction Writing

The following writing forms are presented in this book to provide students with a variety of real-world and academic formats and purposes for writing.

Expository Writing

Biography: a true story about a person's life, giving important information about the person and describing major events in the order in which they happened

Descriptive Paragraph: a paragraph that describes a person, place, thing, or event, using vivid details so the reader can easily imagine it

Directions: a paragraph that tells readers how to make or do something

News Article: a report that gives factual information about a current event and answers *who, what, where, when, why,* and *how* about the event

Research Report: a report that gives details and facts about a topic, using information gathered from different sources

Response to Literature: writing that responds to a prompt, or question, about a specific reading selection

Summary: a short piece of writing that gives the main idea and the most important details about a longer piece of writing, such as a story or book

Persuasive Writing

Persuasive Letter: a letter written to persuade someone to agree with a certain idea or to take a specific action

Persuasive Paragraph: a paragraph written to persuade others to agree with the writer or to take a specific action

Review: a piece of writing that gives important information and expresses an opinion about a book, movie, show, restaurant, or product

Narrative Writing

Creative Nonfiction: a true story that a writer tells, using some of the same strategies writers use when they write fiction

Friendly Letter: a letter that tells about something personal in the writer's life and that is written to someone the writer knows

Journal Entry: a record of someone's personal thoughts and feelings about a topic or event

Personal Narrative: a true story that a writer tells about a specific event or experience from his or her own life

Writing a Paragraph

Name: _____

Paragraph

Introducing a Paragraph
Read this example of a paragraph.

Writing Model

A Happy Hippo Is a Wet Hippo

A hippopotamus, or hippo, is well suited to spend time in the water. A hippo's eyes, ears, and nose are on top of its head. This means that a hippo can see, hear, and breathe while it stays cool in the water. A hippo can hold its breath for as much as five minutes! It also has webbed feet that help it move through water. It's no wonder that a hippo loves water.

Writer's Purpose: <u>to tell how a hippo is able to spend</u>
<u>a lot of time in the water</u>

10 BASICS OF NONFICTION WRITING   Nonfiction Writing • EMC 6012 • © Evan-Moor Corp.

Name: _____

Paragraph

Writing a Topic Sentence

A. Read each paragraph. Check the box next to the best topic sentence to begin the paragraph.

1. _____ They have thick fur to keep them warm. And they blow air bubbles into their fur. The air bubbles help keep otters dry, which keeps them warm.
   - ☑ Otters are able to stay warm in cold ocean water.
   - ☐ Otters are good at blowing bubbles.

2. _____ They are as long as a big airplane! They are bigger than the largest land animal, the elephant. Blue whales are even bigger than the largest dinosaurs that ever lived.
   - ☐ Blue whales are interesting.
   - ☑ Blue whales are the largest animals that ever lived.

3. _____ The largest sharks are as long as a school bus. Small ones are less than a foot long. Most sharks are about 5 to 6 feet long. That is about as long as an adult human is tall.
   - ☐ Some sharks are big.
   - ☑ Sharks come in different sizes.

B. Read each paragraph. Rewrite the underlined sentence so it tells the main idea of the paragraph.

1. <u>Firefighters are brave.</u> Firetrucks take firefighters where they need to go. Firetrucks hold water for putting out fires. Firetrucks also have many tools to help firefighters.

   <u>A firetruck is useful.</u>

2. <u>Giraffes are animals.</u> They are the tallest land animals in the world. Their long necks help them reach the leaves on tall trees. Because of their height, giraffes can look out for danger.

   <u>Giraffes are very tall.</u>

© Evan-Moor Corp. • EMC 6012 • Nonfiction Writing   BASICS OF NONFICTION WRITING 11

Lesson 1 Introducing a Paragraph

A paragraph expresses one main idea. A topic sentence clearly states that idea. Other sentences add supporting details.

1. Display the model of a paragraph on p. 10, "A Happy Hippo Is a Wet Hippo," and say: **A paragraph is a group of sentences about the same subject. This paragraph is about hippos.**

2. Read aloud the paragraph as students follow along. Then ask: **What is the purpose of this paragraph?** (to tell how a hippo is able to spend a lot of time in the water) Have students write the purpose on the lines provided.

3. Invite students to offer opinions about what makes this a good paragraph. Prompt students by asking: **Is the topic of the paragraph clear? Does the first sentence tell about the topic? Are all of the sentences about that topic?**

4. Explain that students will use the model as they study the skills needed to write a good paragraph.

➤ **Extend the Lesson:** Have students read paragraphs in science or social studies textbooks and identify the topic of each paragraph.

Lesson 2 Writing a Topic Sentence

1. Remind students that all of the sentences in a paragraph should be about one main idea. Introduce the concept of a topic sentence: Say: **A topic sentence tells what the paragraph is mostly about. It gives the *main idea* of the paragraph.**

2. Reread "A Happy Hippo Is a Wet Hippo" and ask: **Which sentence tells you what the paragraph is mostly about?** *(A hippopotamus, or hippo, is well suited to spend time in the water.)* Have students underline the sentence. Point out that this is the topic sentence.

3. Read the directions for Activity A on p. 11. Read the first paragraph and explain: **This paragraph is about otters. All of the sentences are about how otters stay warm. The first choice is a better topic sentence:** *Otters are able to stay warm in cold ocean water.* **Not all of the paragraph is about otters blowing bubbles.** Then have students complete the activity in pairs.

4. For Activity B, read aloud the directions and complete the first item as a group. Then have students complete the second item independently. Review the answers.

➤ **Extend the Lesson:** Have students write topic sentences about penguins or other animals.

Lesson 3 Using Good Details

1. Review the qualities of a good paragraph. Say: **The topic sentence tells what the paragraph is about. Other sentences give details about the topic.**

2. Remind students that the first sentence of "A Happy Hippo Is a Wet Hippo" tells what the paragraph is about. Read the remaining sentences slowly and have students raise their hands if they hear a detail about how hippos are able to stay in water for a long time. Point out that all of the sentences give details about the topic. Say: **Good details tell only about the main idea.**

3. Read the directions for Activity A on p. 12. Then read the topic of item 1. Say: **Look for details that tell about sloths being slow. If you find a detail that does not tell about sloths being slow, cross it out.** Have students complete the activity independently.

4. Read the directions for Activity B. Have a volunteer read aloud the topic sentence for item 1. Ask: **Why might dogs be considered good pets?** Explain that those reasons can become good details for the topic sentence. Have students complete the activity independently or in pairs. Encourage students to express each detail as a complete sentence. Invite students to share their answers.

➤ **Extend the Lesson:** Have students write two or more details for the topic sentences they wrote in the Lesson 2 extension activity.

Lesson 4 Reviewing a Paragraph

1. Review the qualities of a good paragraph: a topic sentence that tells what the paragraph is about and detail sentences that support the topic sentence.

2. Read aloud "Big Pigs" on p. 13 as students follow along. Guide them through revising the draft. Explain that the paragraph is mostly about what pigs look like. Ask: **How can we fix the topic sentence?** Prompt students to suggest a topic sentence that is appropriate. (e.g., Pigs look interesting.) Ask: **Which sentence does not tell how pigs look?** (There is a fairy tale about three pigs and a wolf.) Say: **Cross out this sentence, because it does not belong in the paragraph.** Ask: **What details could you add about how pigs look?** (e.g., They have curly tails, flat noses, floppy ears.) Guide students to add sentences that provide good details.

3. Have students write their revisions on a separate sheet of paper. Invite volunteers to share their paragraphs.

BASICS OF NONFICTION WRITING   **9**

Page 12 / Student Book Page 4

Name: _____   Paragraph

Using Good Details

A. Read each paragraph. Notice the details. Cross out the detail that does not tell more about the main idea.

1. **Topic:** a slow-moving animal

   Sloths are slow creatures. They live mostly in trees and do not move very much. ~~They have claws.~~ They chew leaves slowly. They even blink slowly.

2. **Topic:** plant parts

   A plant has three parts. One part is the leaves. ~~Some plants grow tall.~~ Another part is the stem. The part under the ground is the roots.

3. **Topic:** a water bird

   Ducks live near water. Their feathers keep them dry. ~~Geese and swans also live near water.~~ Ducks have webbed feet that help them swim. They eat fish, water snails, and other things.

B. Write two good details for each topic sentence.

1. **Topic sentence:** Dogs are good pets.

   Details: They can do tricks.
   They are playful.

2. **Topic sentence:** Elephants are not good pets.

   Details: They eat too much.
   They do not fit in the car.

3. **Topic sentence:** Fish are easy pets to keep.

   Details: They only need food and a clean tank.
   They do not need walks.

12   **BASICS OF NONFICTION WRITING**   Nonfiction Writing • EMC 6012 • © Evan-Moor Corp.

Page 13 and Sample Revision / Student Book Page 5

Name: _____   Paragraph

Reviewing a Paragraph

Revise this paragraph. Use what you have learned to make it stronger. Write your paragraph on a separate sheet of paper.

Focu...

Sample Answer

Big Pigs

Pigs are funny-looking animals. They have short legs and small eyes. Their ears are floppy. Their noses are flat. They have curly tails. Some pigs are pink. Some pigs are black. Some have dark spots on white skin.

Name: _____

Introducing a Paragraph

Read this example of a paragraph.

Writing Model

A Happy Hippo Is a Wet Hippo

A hippopotamus, or hippo, is well suited to spend time in the water. A hippo's eyes, ears, and nose are on top of its head. This means that a hippo can see, hear, and breathe while it stays cool in the water. A hippo can hold its breath for as much as five minutes! It also has webbed feet that help it move through water. It's no wonder that a hippo loves water.

Writer's Purpose: _____

_____

Writing a Topic Sentence

A. Read each paragraph. Check the box next to the best topic sentence to begin the paragraph.

1. _____ They have thick fur to keep them warm. And they blow air bubbles into their fur. The air bubbles help keep otters dry, which keeps them warm.

   ☐ Otters are able to stay warm in cold ocean water.
   ☐ Otters are good at blowing bubbles.

2. _____ They are as long as a big airplane! They are bigger than the largest land animal, the elephant. Blue whales are even bigger than the largest dinosaurs that ever lived.

   ☐ Blue whales are interesting.
   ☐ Blue whales are the largest animals that ever lived.

3. _____ The largest sharks are as long as a school bus. Small ones are less than a foot long. Most sharks are about 5 to 6 feet long. That is about as long as an adult human is tall.

   ☐ Some sharks are big.
   ☐ Sharks come in different sizes.

B. Read each paragraph. Rewrite the underlined sentence so it tells the main idea of the paragraph.

1. Firefighters are brave. Firetrucks take firefighters where they need to go. Firetrucks hold water for putting out fires. Firetrucks also have many tools to help firefighters.

   _____

2. Giraffes are animals. They are the tallest land animals in the world. Their long necks help them reach the leaves on tall trees. Because of their height, giraffes can look out for danger.

   _____

Using Good Details

A. Read each paragraph. Notice the details. Cross out the detail that does not tell more about the main idea.

1. **Topic:** a slow-moving animal

   Sloths are slow creatures. They live mostly in trees and do not move very much. They have claws. They chew leaves slowly. They even blink slowly.

2. **Topic:** plant parts

   A plant has three parts. One part is the leaves. Some plants grow tall. Another part is the stem. The part under the ground is the roots.

3. **Topic:** a water bird

   Ducks live near water. Their feathers keep them dry. Geese and swans also live near water. Ducks have webbed feet that help them swim. They eat fish, water snails, and other things.

B. Write two good details for each topic sentence.

1. **Topic sentence:** Dogs are good pets.

   Details: _____

   _____

2. **Topic sentence:** Elephants are not good pets.

   Details: _____

   _____

3. **Topic sentence:** Fish are easy pets to keep.

   Details: _____

   _____

Reviewing a Paragraph

Revise this paragraph. Use what you have learned to make it stronger.
Write your paragraph on a separate sheet of paper.

Focus on:
- ✓ writing a sentence that tells the main idea
- ✓ using details that tell more about the main idea

Draft

Big Pigs

Pigs are good animals. They have short legs and small eyes. Their tails are curly. There is a fairy tale about three pigs and a wolf. Some pigs are pink. Some pigs are black. Some have dark spots on white skin.

Writing to Show Sequence

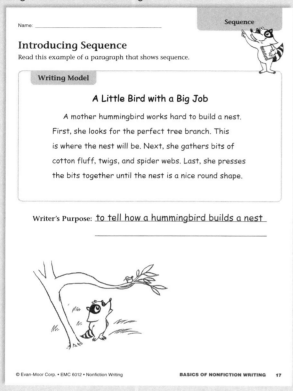

Lesson 1 Introducing Sequence

Writing that shows sequence usually identifies steps in a process or tells about a series of events using chronological order and order words.

1. Tell students that the word *sequence* means "order." Say: **When you write about something that happened, it is important for the steps or events to be in the right sequence, or order.** Then act out four steps for brushing teeth and announce the action prior to acting it out. Use the signal words *first, next, then,* and *last.* (e.g., First, put toothpaste on your toothbrush. Next, brush all of your teeth on the bottom and the top. Then rinse your mouth with water. Last, put your toothbrush away.) Say: **Using the correct sequence makes your writing easy for readers to follow and understand.**

2. Read aloud "A Little Bird with a Big Job" on p. 17 as students follow along. Ask: **What is this paragraph about?** (a hummingbird making a nest) Have students identify the topic sentence in the model. *(A mother hummingbird works hard to build a nest.)*

3. Ask: **What is the purpose of this paragraph?** (to tell how a hummingbird builds a nest) Have students write the purpose on the lines provided.

4. Invite students to offer opinions about what makes this a good example of writing to show sequence. Prompt students by asking: **Does the paragraph tell the events in order? Does it include words that tell you what happened first, next, and last?**

5. Explain that students will use the model as they study the skills needed to write a good paragraph.

➤ **Extend the Lesson:** Have partners describe to each other how they get ready for bed most nights. Remind them to tell the steps in the order that they happen.

Lesson 2 Showing Sequence

1. Say: **When you write to show sequence, you tell about the events in time order, or the order that they happened.**

2. Point out that the paragraph on p. 17 uses time order. Have students number each step in building a nest. Ask: **What does the mother bird do first?** (look for a good branch) Say: **Label this step 1.** Ask: **What does she do after that?** (gather bits of stuff) Say: **Label this step 2.** Continue guiding students through the last step.

3. Direct students to Activity A on p. 18. Say: **These drawings show the sequence of a frog's life cycle, but they are not in the correct order.** Build background as needed by discussing each life cycle stage (adult frog, eggs, froglet, tadpole). Have students work in pairs to number the drawings in order.

4. Read aloud the instructions for Activity B. Explain that the out-of-order sentences are about a boy who goes fishing. Then read the sentences aloud. Have students work in small groups to write the sentences in order in the chart.

➤ **Extend the Lesson:** Have students copy the chart from Activity B and use it to show the sequence for a common activity, such as putting on socks and shoes, leaving the classroom in an orderly manner, playing hopscotch, or feeding a pet.

Lesson 3 Using Order Words

1. Say: **To show sequence, writers often use words such as *first*, *next*, *then*, *last*, and *finally* to tell when things happen. These are called *order words*.** Give the first step in a familiar process, such as making a peanut butter sandwich. Say: **First, get two slices of bread.** Invite two or three students to continue the process, starting each step with an order word.

2. Have students find and circle the order words in "A Little Bird with a Big Job." Point out that the order words help focus readers on the individual steps in the sequence.

3. Read aloud the directions on p. 19 and use the first item to model the activity. Say: **The bear fell asleep *after* it yawned. So I can say "First, the bear yawned." The next sentence will begin with *Then*.** Have students complete the activity independently. Review the answers as a class.

➤ **Extend the Lesson:** Have students look for order words in textbook passages.

Lesson 4 Putting Sentences in Order

1. Remind students that writers often use order words to indicate the sequence of events. Prompt them to give examples of order words: *first, next, then, last, finally.*

2. Review the model on p. 17 and read aloud the first sentence. Say: **This sentence tells what the paragraph is mostly about. The sentences that follow give details about how a mother hummingbird builds a nest. The details are in time order.**

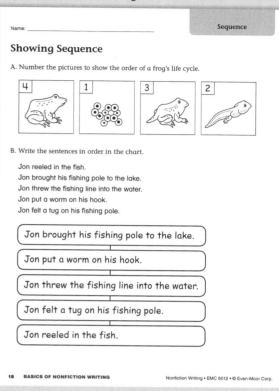

Page 20 / Student Book Page 10

Name: _____

Sequence

Putting Sentences in Order

A. Number the sentences to show the correct order.

__3__ Next, she chases away other hummingbirds until the eggs hatch.

__2__ First, she sits on the eggs to keep them warm.

__4__ Then, after the eggs hatch, she finds food for the babies.

__5__ Last, she feeds the babies about every ten minutes.

__1__ A mother hummingbird cares for her babies until they can fly.

B. Now write the sentences as a paragraph. Put them in the correct order.

A mother hummingbird cares for her babies until they can fly. First, she sits on the eggs to keep them warm. Next, she chases away other hummingbirds until the eggs hatch. Then, after the eggs hatch, she finds food for the babies. Last, she feeds the babies about every ten minutes.

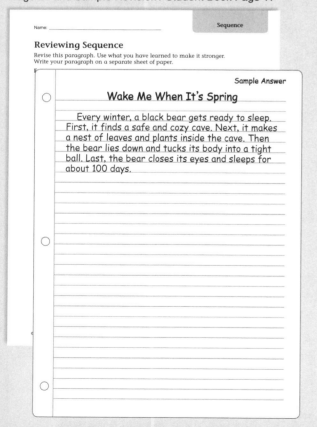

20   BASICS OF NONFICTION WRITING   Nonfiction Writing • EMC 6012 • © Evan-Moor Corp.

Page 21 and Sample Revision / Student Book Page 11

Name: _____

Sequence

Reviewing Sequence

Revise this paragraph. Use what you have learned to make it stronger.
Write your paragraph on a separate sheet of paper.

Sample Answer

Wake Me When It's Spring

Every winter, a black bear gets ready to sleep. First, it finds a safe and cozy cave. Next, it makes a nest of leaves and plants inside the cave. Then the bear lies down and tucks its body into a tight ball. Last, the bear closes its eyes and sleeps for about 100 days.

---

3. Read the directions for Activity A on p. 20. Explain that the sentences, which are not in order, describe how a mother hummingbird takes care of her babies. Have students complete the activity independently or in pairs. Review the answers and ask students to explain how they determined the sequence.

4. Have students complete Activity B independently and then practice reading their paragraphs to a partner.

➤ **Extend the Lesson:** Provide mixed-up paragraphs as sentence strips and have students arrange or write the sentences in order.

Lesson 5 Reviewing Sequence

1. Review the qualities of a paragraph that shows sequence: a topic sentence, sentences that show time order, and order words.

2. Read aloud "Wake Me When It's Spring" on p. 21 as students follow along. Guide students through revising the draft. Ask: **What is the main idea of the paragraph?** (A black bear gets ready to sleep for the winter.) **Is there one sentence that tells the main idea?** (Yes. *Every winter, a black bear gets ready to sleep.*) Say: **This is a good topic sentence for the paragraph. Let's begin the paragraph with this sentence.** Then ask: **Do the sentences tell the events in order?** (no) **What would a bear do first to prepare for winter?** (find a safe place) **Then what would the bear do?** (make a nest inside the cave) When students have determined the events, help them look for sentences that match. Then prompt them to put the sentences in order. Remind students to add order words to clarify the sequence.

3. Have students write their revisions on a separate sheet of paper. Invite volunteers to read their revised sequence paragraphs aloud.

Name: _____

Introducing Sequence

Read this example of a paragraph that shows sequence.

Writing Model

A Little Bird with a Big Job

A mother hummingbird works hard to build a nest. First, she looks for the perfect tree branch. This is where the nest will be. Next, she gathers bits of cotton fluff, twigs, and spider webs. Last, she presses the bits together until the nest is a nice round shape.

Writer's Purpose: _____

_____

Showing Sequence

A. Number the pictures to show the order of a frog's life cycle.

 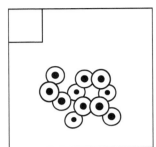  

B. Write the sentences in order in the chart.

Jon reeled in the fish.

Jon brought his fishing pole to the lake.

Jon threw the fishing line into the water.

Jon put a worm on his hook.

Jon felt a tug on his fishing pole.

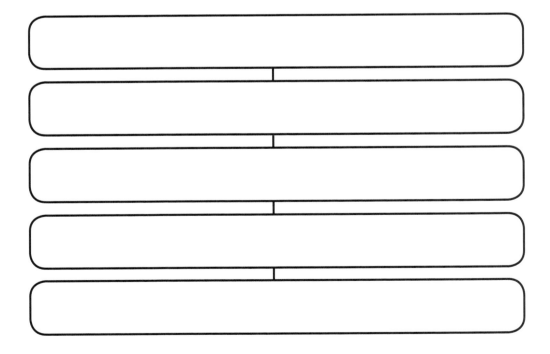

Using Order Words

Complete each sentence, using the best order word.

1. _____, the bear yawned. _____ it fell asleep.

   First Then

2. _____, Amy walked home. _____ she changed her clothes.

   First Then

3. Matt made his bed. _____ he ate breakfast. _____, he brushed his teeth.

   Last Then

4. Jada got ready for school. _____, she got dressed. _____, she gathered her books. Then she packed her lunch.

   First Next

5. Puff had an adventure. First, he climbed the neighbor's tree. _____ he got stuck. _____, he came home.

   Later Then

6. Lea got a piece of clay. She shaped it into a bowl. _____, she let it dry. _____, she painted it.

   Next Last

7. _____, Noah pulled his snow pants over his jeans. _____, he put on his jacket. Then he put on his warm hat. _____, he pushed his hands into his gloves.

   Next Last First

8. The dog carried a bone into the yard. He dropped it so he could dig a hole. _____, he put the bone into the hole. _____, he filled the hole with dirt. _____, he dug up the bone.

   Later Next Then

Putting Sentences in Order

A. Number the sentences to show the correct order.

_____ Next, she chases away other hummingbirds until the eggs hatch.

_____ First, she sits on the eggs to keep them warm.

_____ Then, after the eggs hatch, she finds food for the babies.

_____ Last, she feeds the babies about every ten minutes.

_____ A mother hummingbird cares for her babies until they can fly.

B. Now write the sentences as a paragraph. Put them in the correct order.

_____

_____

_____

_____

_____

_____

Reviewing Sequence

Revise this paragraph. Use what you have learned to make it stronger. Write your paragraph on a separate sheet of paper.

Focus on:

✓ writing a sentence that tells the main idea
✓ showing events in the order that they happen
✓ using signal words to show the sequence

Draft

Wake Me When It's Spring

The bear lies down and tucks its body into a tight ball. Every winter, a black bear gets ready to sleep. It finds a safe and cozy cave. The bear closes its eyes and sleeps for about 100 days. It makes a nest of leaves and plants inside the cave.

Writing to Show Cause and Effect

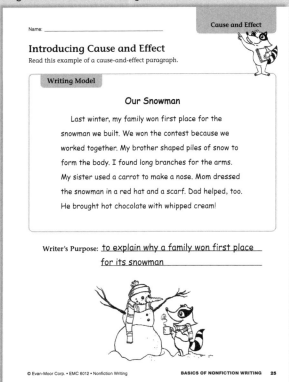

Lesson 1 Introducing Cause and Effect

A cause-and-effect paragraph tells what happens and why it happens. The topic sentence tells the cause-and-effect relationship. Details support the topic sentence and tell more about the cause or the effect.

1. Draw two boxes, side by side, on the board, with an arrow connecting them. Label the first box *cause* and the second box *effect*. Demonstrate the concept of cause and effect by removing a pushpin from a piece of paper on a bulletin board and allowing the paper to slip to the floor. Ask: **What happened?** (The paper fell.) **What caused it to fall?** (removing the pin) Write each response in the appropriate box on the board. Repeat with other simple actions.

2. Then explain: **An *effect* is something that happens. A *cause* is why it happens.**

3. Read "Our Snowman" on p. 25 as students follow along. Ask: **What is the purpose of this cause-and-effect paragraph?** (to explain why a family won first place for its snowman) Have students write the purpose on the lines provided.

4. Invite students to offer opinions about what makes this a good example of writing to show cause and effect. Prompt students by asking: **Does the paragraph name something that happens and explain why it happens? Does the paragraph give details that tell more about what happened?**

5. Explain that students will use the model as they study the skills needed to write cause-and-effect paragraphs.

➤ **Extend the Lesson:** Provide additional samples of cause-and-effect paragraphs and have students practice telling the purpose of each paragraph.

Lesson 2 Showing Causes and Effects

1. Remind students that an *effect* is something that happens and a *cause* is why it happens.

2. Draw and label a cause-and-effect graphic organizer as in Lesson 1. Review the model on p. 25 and explain that the topic sentence identifies a cause and its effect. Read aloud the topic sentence: *We won the contest because we worked together.* Ask: **What did the family do?** (They won the contest.) Record the answer in the *effect* box on the board. Then ask: **Why did the family win?** (because they worked together) Record the answer in the *cause* box on the board.

3. Read aloud the directions for Activity A on p. 26. Guide students through the first item by asking: **What happened?** (Brady put on his hat.) **Why did he put on his hat?** (because it was cold) Then have students complete the activity in small groups. Review the answers as a class.

4. Have students complete Activity B in pairs. If necessary, model the activity using the first item. When students have completed the activity, invite volunteers to share their sentences with the class.

➤ **Extend the Lesson:** Have students complete these sentences to show cause and effect: *When I see ____, I always laugh. If I ____, then I will get a good grade.*

Lesson 3 Using Signal Words

1. Say: **When writers tell about causes and effects, they can use words such as *so* and *because* in their sentences. These words signal causes and effects.**

2. Read this sentence from "Our Snowman," emphasizing the signal word in the sentence: *We won the contest because we worked together.* Say: **The word *because* is a clue.** Ask: **Why did the family win the contest?** (*because* the family members worked together)

3. Read aloud the directions for Activity A on p. 27. Use the example to model the activity. Say: **I need to figure out which sentence in this example gives the cause and which gives the effect. Then I will put the two sentences together using the signal word *so*.** Point out that when you use *so* to join sentences, you often put a comma after the word that comes before *so*. Explain that this is also true when you use *because*. Have students complete the activity independently. Review the answers together.

4. For Activity B, guide students in brainstorming topics for cause-and-effect sentences, about animals. (e.g., Petting a cat may cause it to purr. Birds fly south when the weather turns cold.) Then have students complete the activity independently. Invite volunteers to share their sentences.

➤ **Extend the Lesson:** Present other words and phrases that can signal cause and effect, such as *if … then; since; when; before, after.* Have students practice using these words in sentences.

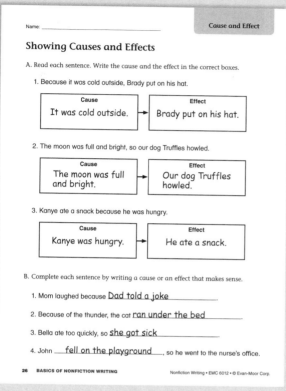

Page 26 / Student Book Page 14

Name: _____ Cause and Effect

Showing Causes and Effects

A. Read each sentence. Write the cause and the effect in the correct boxes.

1. Because it was cold outside, Brady put on his hat.

Cause		Effect
It was cold outside.	→	Brady put on his hat.

2. The moon was full and bright, so our dog Truffles howled.

Cause		Effect
The moon was full and bright.	→	Our dog Truffles howled.

3. Kanye ate a snack because he was hungry.

Cause		Effect
Kanye was hungry.	→	He ate a snack.

B. Complete each sentence by writing a cause or an effect that makes sense.

1. Mom laughed because **Dad told a joke**.

2. Because of the thunder, the cat **ran under the bed**.

3. Bella ate too quickly, so **she got sick**.

4. John **fell on the playground**, so he went to the nurse's office.

26　BASICS OF NONFICTION WRITING　　Nonfiction Writing • EMC 6012 • © Evan-Moor Corp.

Page 27 / Student Book Page 15

Name: _____ Cause and Effect

Using Signal Words

A. Combine each pair of sentences to show cause and effect. Use the signal word in bold.

Example
Bees need to protect their hive. They sting animals that come near it. (**so**)
Bees need to protect their hive, so they sting
animals that come near it.

1. Worms have no bones. They can squirm. (**so**)
Worms have no bones, so they can squirm.

2. Horses run fast. They have strong legs. (**because**)
Horses run fast because they have strong legs.

3. Tigers see well. They can hunt at night. (**so**)
Tigers see well, so they can hunt at night.

4. A mole can dig. Its claws are sharp. (**because**)
A mole can dig because its claws are sharp.

5. The owl is white. It can hide in the snow. (**so**)
The owl is white, so it can hide in the snow.

6. A cat moves quietly. Its paws are padded. (**because**)
A cat moves quietly because its paws are padded.

B. Write a sentence about an animal. Tell about a cause and an effect. Use **so** or **because**.

My dog wagged her tail because she was happy.

© Evan-Moor Corp. • EMC 6012 • Nonfiction Writing　　BASICS OF NONFICTION WRITING　27

Page 28 / Student Book Page 16

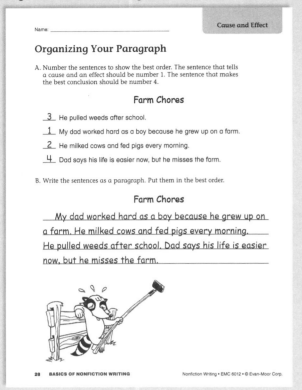

> Name: _____
>
> Cause and Effect
>
> ## Organizing Your Paragraph
>
> A. Number the sentences to show the best order. The sentence that tells a cause and an effect should be number 1. The sentence that makes the best conclusion should be number 4.
>
> ### Farm Chores
>
> __3__ He pulled weeds after school.
>
> __1__ My dad worked hard as a boy because he grew up on a farm.
>
> __2__ He milked cows and fed pigs every morning.
>
> __4__ Dad says his life is easier now, but he misses the farm.
>
> B. Write the sentences as a paragraph. Put them in the best order.
>
> ### Farm Chores
>
> My dad worked hard as a boy because he grew up on a farm. He milked cows and fed pigs every morning. He pulled weeds after school. Dad says his life is easier now, but he misses the farm.
>
> 28   BASICS OF NONFICTION WRITING   Nonfiction Writing • EMC 6012 • © Evan-Moor Corp.

Page 29 and Sample Revision / Student Book Page 17

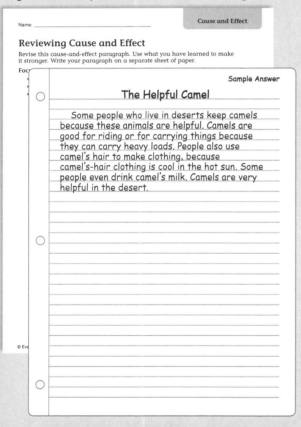

> Name: _____
>
> Cause and Effect
>
> ## Reviewing Cause and Effect
>
> Revise this cause-and-effect paragraph. Use what you have learned to make it stronger. Write your paragraph on a separate sheet of paper.
>
> Foc
>
> Sample Answer
>
> ### The Helpful Camel
>
> Some people who live in deserts keep camels because these animals are helpful. Camels are good for riding or for carrying things because they can carry heavy loads. People also use camel's hair to make clothing, because camel's-hair clothing is cool in the hot sun. Some people even drink camel's milk. Camels are very helpful in the desert.

Lesson 4 Organizing Your Paragraph

1. Say: **Good organization makes your writing clearer. It helps readers understand what you are saying.**

2. Call students' attention to the first sentence on p. 25. Point out that it tells what happened. Then remind students that the next sentence is the topic sentence. Explain that it repeats what happened, tells why, and tells what the paragraph is mostly about. Read the last sentence and explain how it concludes the paragraph. Say: **This sentence tells one last thing about the family's time together. The other sentences give details about how everyone in the family helped build the snowman.**

3. Direct students to p. 28. Read the instructions for Activity A and have volunteers read aloud the sentences under the title "Farm Chores." Ask: **What are these sentences about?** (working on a farm) Clarify that a good conclusion often restates the ideas in the topic sentence. Help students identify the topic sentence (*My dad worked hard …*) and the conclusion (*Dad says his life is easier …*). Have students complete the activity in pairs. Then review the answers as a class.

4. Have students complete Activity B independently. Invite a volunteer to read aloud the paragraph.

➤ **Extend the Lesson:** Choose one of the sentences from Activity A on p. 27. Guide students in writing two sentences that provide more detail and a conclusion.

Lesson 5 Reviewing Cause and Effect

1. Review the qualities of a cause-and-effect paragraph: a topic sentence that tells something that happened and explains why, words that signal cause and effect, and clear organization.

2. Read aloud "The Helpful Camel" on p. 29 as students follow along. Guide them through revising the draft. Ask: **Why do people who live in the desert keep camels?** (because camels are helpful) Prompt students to combine the first two sentences, using the signal word *because*. Then read this sentence aloud: *Camels can carry heavy loads.* Ask: **Where does this sentence belong?** (after *Camels are good for riding …*) Prompt students to combine the two sentences, using *because*. Then prompt them to find two other sentences to combine. (*People also use camel's hair …* and *Camel's-hair clothing …*)

3. Have students write their revisions on a separate sheet of paper. Invite volunteers to share their paragraphs.

Name: _____

Introducing Cause and Effect

Read this example of a cause-and-effect paragraph.

Writing Model

Our Snowman

Last winter, my family won first place for the snowman we built. We won the contest because we worked together. My brother shaped piles of snow to form the body. I found long branches for the arms. My sister used a carrot to make a nose. Mom dressed the snowman in a red hat and a scarf. Dad helped, too. He brought hot chocolate with whipped cream!

Writer's Purpose: _____

_____

Showing Causes and Effects

A. Read each sentence. Write the cause and the effect in the correct boxes.

1. Because it was cold outside, Brady put on his hat.

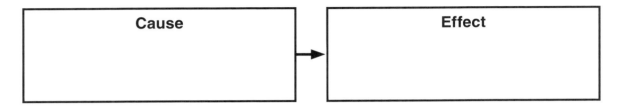

2. The moon was full and bright, so our dog Truffles howled.

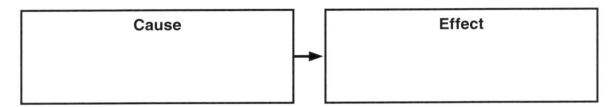

3. Kanye ate a snack because he was hungry.

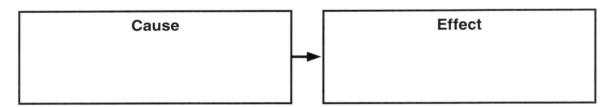

B. Complete each sentence by writing a cause or an effect that makes sense.

1. Mom laughed because _____.

2. Because of the thunder, the cat _____.

3. Bella ate too quickly, so _____.

4. John _____, so he went to the nurse's office.

Using Signal Words

A. Combine each pair of sentences to show cause and effect. Use the signal word in bold.

> **Example**
>
> Bees need to protect their hive. They sting animals that come near it. (**so**)
>
> <u>Bees need to protect their hive, so they sting</u>
> <u>animals that come near it.</u>

1. Worms have no bones. They can squirm. (**so**)

   _____

2. Horses run fast. They have strong legs. (**because**)

   _____

3. Tigers see well. They can hunt at night. (**so**)

   _____

4. A mole can dig. Its claws are sharp. (**because**)

   _____

5. The owl is white. It can hide in the snow. (**so**)

   _____

6. A cat moves quietly. Its paws are padded. (**because**)

   _____

B. Write a sentence about an animal. Tell about a cause and an effect. Use **so** or **because**.

_____

Organizing Your Paragraph

A. Number the sentences to show the best order. The sentence that tells a cause and an effect should be number **1**. The sentence that makes the best conclusion should be number **4**.

Farm Chores

____ He pulled weeds after school.

____ My dad worked hard as a boy because he grew up on a farm.

____ He milked cows and fed pigs every morning.

____ Dad says his life is easier now, but he misses the farm.

B. Write the sentences as a paragraph. Put them in the best order.

Farm Chores

_____

_____

_____

_____

Name: _____

Reviewing Cause and Effect

Revise this cause-and-effect paragraph. Use what you have learned to make it stronger. Write your paragraph on a separate sheet of paper.

Focus on:

✓ writing a sentence that tells a cause and an effect
✓ using a signal word to tell a cause and an effect
✓ putting your sentences in order so that they make sense

Draft

The Helpful Camel

Some people who live in deserts keep camels. These animals are helpful in several ways. Camels are good for riding or for carrying things. People also use camel's hair to make clothing. Camels can carry heavy loads. Some people even drink camel's milk. Camel's-hair clothing is cool in the hot sun. Camels are very helpful in the desert.

Writing to Compare and Contrast

Page 33 / Student Book Page 19

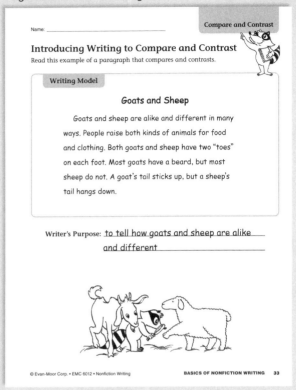

Introducing Writing to Compare and Contrast

Writing that compares and contrasts shows how two or more things are alike or different.

1. Ask students to think of two things that are mostly alike, such as a pen and a pencil. Say: **If you wanted to tell how they are alike and different, you would compare and contrast them.** Explain to students that *compare* means to tell how things are alike and *contrast* means to tell how they are different.

2. Read aloud "Goats and Sheep" on p. 33 as students follow along. Have students identify the topic sentence. *(Goats and sheep are alike and different in many ways.)* Point out that the topic sentence tells what the paragraph compares and contrasts.

3. Ask: **What is the purpose of this paragraph?** (to tell how goats and sheep are alike and different) Have students write the purpose on the lines provided.

4. Invite students to offer opinions about what makes this a good example of writing to compare and contrast. Prompt students by asking: **Does the first sentence tell what the paragraph will compare and contrast? Does the paragraph tell how goats and sheep are alike and different?**

➤ **Extend the Lesson:** Have students make lists of animals that they could easily compare and contrast (e.g., horses and zebras).

Page 34 / Student Book Page 20

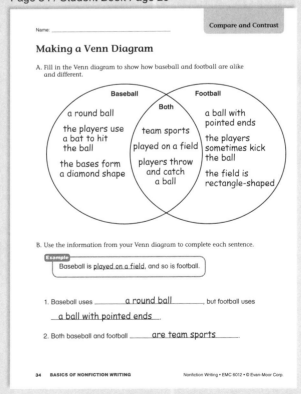

Lesson 2 Making a Venn Diagram

1. Draw a Venn diagram on the board. Label the circles *Goats* and *Sheep* and the overlapping area *Both*. Review the model on p. 33 and ask: **How are goats and sheep different?** Elicit responses and record the information in the diagram. (Goats: tail sticks up, beard. Sheep: tail hangs down, no beard.) Ask: **How are they alike?** (Both: two-toed feet, raised for food and clothing)

2. Say: **You can use a Venn diagram to record your ideas when you compare and contrast two things.** Read the directions for Activity A on p. 34 and have students fill in the Venn diagram in pairs.

3. Have students complete Activity B independently. Ask volunteers to share their sentences.

➤ **Extend the Lesson:** Have students make Venn diagrams to compare and contrast two animals from the list they generated in the Lesson 1 extension activity.

Lesson 3 Using Signal Words

1. Read aloud this sentence from the writing model on p. 33: *Both goats and sheep have two "toes" on each foot.* Say: **The word** *both* **tells me that this sentence is making a comparison. It shows one way that sheep are similar to goats.** Write the words *alike* and *both* on the board and discuss how they signal comparisons.

2. Read aloud this sentence: *Most goats have a beard, but most sheep do not.* Say: **The writer is pointing out one difference between goats and sheep. The word** *but* **tells me that this sentence is contrasting goats and sheep.** Write the signal words *but* and *different* on the board and explain: **You can use these signal words when you want to contrast two or more things.**

3. Have students work in small groups to find and circle the signal words in the writing model. Review their findings as a group.

4. Read aloud the directions for Activity A on p. 35. Clarify that the words in the box can be used more than once. Read the first item and ask: **Is this sentence about how lions and tigers are alike or different?** (alike) **How do you know?** (It says "they are big cats." That's one way they are alike.) Have students try different signal words in the sentence until they find one that is suitable. Then have students complete the activity in pairs.

5. Have students complete Activity B in small groups. Invite volunteers to share their sentences.

➤ **Extend the Lesson:** Introduce additional signal words, such as *however* and *too,* and give students an opportunity to practice using those words.

Lesson 4 Organizing Your Paragraph

1. Say: **A paragraph that compares and contrasts has a topic sentence and detail sentences. It may also have a concluding sentence.**

2. Remind students that a topic sentence in a paragraph that compares and contrasts identifies what is being compared and contrasted. Read the first sentence of the writing model on p. 33 and say: **We can tell that the writer is going to compare and contrast goats and sheep in this paragraph.**

Name: _____   Compare and Contrast

Using Signal Words

A. Complete each sentence by writing a signal word. Use the words in the box.

alike	both	but	different

1. Tigers and lions are ___alike___ because they are big cats.

2. A tiger has stripes, ___but___ a lion does not.

3. Lions and tigers ___both___ roar loudly.

4. A lion's golden fur is ___different___ from a tiger's black and orange fur.

5. ___Both___ lions and tigers eat meat.

6. Lions live in groups, ___but___ tigers live alone.

B. Answer each question by writing a sentence that uses the signal word in bold.

1. What is the same about hot dogs and hamburgers? (**both**)
   Hamburgers and hot dogs both taste good.

2. What is different about winter and spring? (**but**)
   It is cold in winter but warm in spring.

3. What is the same about milk and water? (**alike**)
   Milk and water are alike because they are things that you drink.

© Evan-Moor Corp. • EMC 6012 • Nonfiction Writing   BASICS OF NONFICTION WRITING   35

Page 36 / Student Book Page 22

Name: _____

Compare and Contrast

Organizing Your Paragraph

A. Number the sentences to show the best order for a paragraph.

Ducks and Chickens

__4__ Chicken feathers are softer than duck feathers.

__2__ Ducks and chickens both lay eggs.

__1__ Ducks and chickens are alike, but they are also different.

__3__ Both kinds of birds have wings and feathers.

__5__ Ducks can fly better than chickens can.

B. Write the sentences as a paragraph.

Ducks and Chickens

Ducks and chickens are alike, but they are also different. Ducks and chickens both lay eggs. Both kinds of birds have wings and feathers. Chicken feathers are softer than duck feathers. Ducks can fly better than chickens can.

36   BASICS OF NONFICTION WRITING   Nonfiction Writing • EMC 6012 • © Evan-Moor Corp.

Page 37 and Sample Revision / Student Book Page 23

Name: _____

Compare and Contrast

Reviewing Writing to Compare and Contrast

Revise this paragraph. Use what you have learned to make it stronger.
Write your paragraph on a separate sheet of paper.

Sample Answer

Moths and Butterflies

Even though moths and butterflies look alike, they are different. Moths are insects. Butterflies are insects, too. They both have wings. However, butterflies are more colorful than moths. A butterfly has a smooth body, but a moth has a fuzzy body. Butterflies fly during the day, but moths fly mostly at night.

---

3. Say: **The details in the next few sentences tell how goats and sheep are alike and different.** Point out that the details that compare goats and sheep are together in the paragraph, and the details that contrast the animals are together.

4. Direct students to Activity A on p. 36. Have volunteers read aloud the sentences, one at a time. Ask: **Which sentence compares and contrasts ducks and chickens?** (Ducks and chickens are alike, but they are also different.) Say: **This sentence is a good topic sentence. We can use it to begin our paragraph.** Then say: **One way to organize our detail sentences is to tell about the similarities first and then tell about the differences.** Have students identify and number the sentences accordingly. If they need help deciding how to order the two sentences that compare, point out that one of those sentences (Both kinds of birds have wings and feathers) provides a better link to the sentence that contrasts duck and chicken feathers.

5. Have students complete Activity B independently.

➤ **Extend the Lesson:** Have partners use their completed Venn diagrams from p. 34 as they practice writing to compare and contrast.

Lesson 5 Reviewing Writing to Compare and Contrast

1. Review how to use a Venn diagram. Then review the qualities of writing that compares and contrasts: a topic sentence that expresses a compare-and-contrast relationship, details that tell more about how things are alike and different, and signal words such as *alike, both, same, but,* and *different.*

2. Read aloud "Moths and Butterflies" on p. 37 as students follow along. Then guide students through revising the draft. Ask: **Does the first sentence tell what the paragraph will compare and contrast?** (no) Point out that this sentence might be a good concluding sentence. Read the second and third sentences and ask: **How can we put these sentences together to compare moths and butterflies?** (use the word *both*)

3. Draw a Venn diagram on the board and enlist students' help filling it out to compare butterflies and moths, based on the paragraph.

4. Have students write their revisions on a separate sheet of paper. Invite volunteers to share their paragraphs with the class.

Name: _____

Introducing Writing to Compare and Contrast

Read this example of a paragraph that compares and contrasts.

Writing Model

Goats and Sheep

Goats and sheep are alike and different in many ways. People raise both kinds of animals for food and clothing. Both goats and sheep have two "toes" on each foot. Most goats have a beard, but most sheep do not. A goat's tail sticks up, but a sheep's tail hangs down.

Writer's Purpose: _____

_____

Making a Venn Diagram

A. Fill in the Venn diagram to show how baseball and football are alike and different.

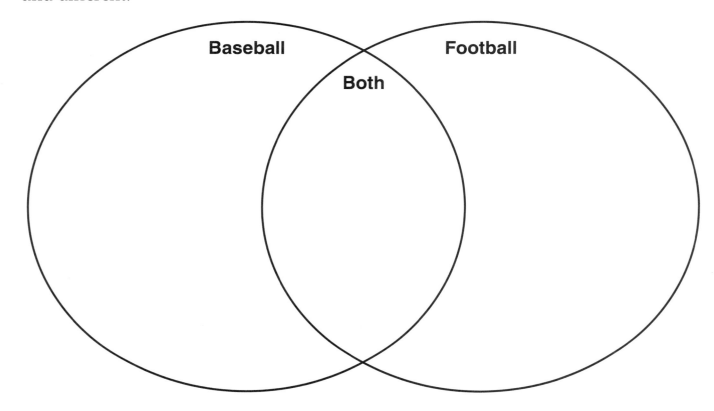

Baseball   **Football**

Both

B. Use the information from your Venn diagram to complete each sentence.

Example

Baseball is <u>played on a field</u>, and so is football.

1. Baseball uses _____, but football uses

_____.

2. Both baseball and football _____.

Name: _____

Using Signal Words

A. Complete each sentence by writing a signal word. Use the words in the box.

alike	both	but	different

1. Tigers and lions are _____ because they are big cats.

2. A tiger has stripes, _____ a lion does not.

3. Lions and tigers _____ roar loudly.

4. A lion's golden fur is _____ from a tiger's black and orange fur.

5. _____ lions and tigers eat meat.

6. Lions live in groups, _____ tigers live alone.

B. Answer each question by writing a sentence that uses the signal word in bold.

1. What is the same about hot dogs and hamburgers? (**both**)

   _____

2. What is different about winter and spring? (**but**)

   _____

3. What is the same about milk and water? (**alike**)

   _____

   _____

Name: _____

Organizing Your Paragraph

A. Number the sentences to show the best order for a paragraph.

Ducks and Chickens

_____ Chicken feathers are softer than duck feathers.

_____ Ducks and chickens both lay eggs.

_____ Ducks and chickens are alike, but they are also different.

_____ Both kinds of birds have wings and feathers.

_____ Ducks can fly better than chickens can.

B. Write the sentences as a paragraph.

Ducks and Chickens

_____

_____

_____

_____

_____

Reviewing Writing to Compare and Contrast

Revise this paragraph. Use what you have learned to make it stronger.
Write your paragraph on a separate sheet of paper.

Focus on:

✓ writing a sentence that tells what is compared and contrasted
✓ adding details about the topic
✓ using words to show that things are alike or different
✓ putting the sentences in order so the paragraph makes sense

Draft

Moths and Butterflies

Moths are insects. Butterflies are
insects. They have wings. Butterflies are
more colorful. A butterfly has a smooth body.
A moth has a fuzzy body. Butterflies fly
during the day, but moths fly mostly at night.

Writing a Summary

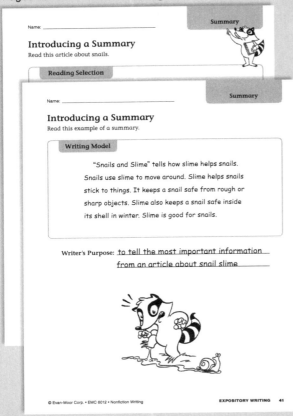

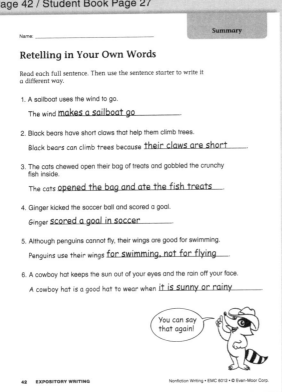

Lesson 1 Introducing a Summary

A summary gives the main idea and the most important details about a longer piece of writing, such as a story or book.

1. Ask students to think of a movie or TV show they saw recently. Say: **If you had only a minute to tell someone about it, you probably would tell the most important or most exciting thing that happened.** Explain that a written summary is similar: It tells the most important information, such as the main idea and supporting details, of a longer piece of writing.

2. Direct students to the article on p. 40, "Snails and Slime." Read aloud the article as students follow along. Then have a volunteer read the summary on p. 41.

3. Ask: **What is the purpose of this summary?** (to tell the most important information from an article about snail slime) Have students write the purpose on the lines provided.

4. Invite students to offer opinions about what makes this a good summary. Prompt students by asking: **Is the summary shorter than the article? Is there one sentence that tells the title and main idea of the article? Did the writer use her own words to tell about the ideas?**

5. Explain that students will use "Snails and Slime" and the writing model as they study the skills needed to write a good summary.

➤ **Extend the Lesson:** Provide other one-paragraph summaries for students to read. Have students identify the main idea in each one.

Lesson 2 Retelling in Your Own Words

1. Review the purpose of a summary. Point out that writers use their own words to retell what someone else has written. Read aloud this sentence from p. 40: *Slime makes it easier for snails to move from place to place.* Ask: **Which sentence on p. 41 retells that idea?** *(Snails use slime to move around.)* Say: **The summary sentence tells the same idea but in different words.**

2. Read aloud the directions on p. 42. Model using the first item. Emphasize that the new sentence should retell the same main idea as the first sentence. Have students complete the activity in pairs.

➤ **Extend the Lesson:** Have students paraphrase sentences from a science or social studies textbook.

Lesson 3 Organizing a Summary

1. Explain that a summary has three parts: The first part is the topic sentence, which names the longer piece of writing that is being summarized; the second part gives important details from the original text; and the third part is a concluding sentence, or ending, that brings the summary to a close.

2. Draw three boxes on the board and label them *Topic Sentence, Details,* and *Ending.* Invite volunteers to copy the sentences from the summary on p. 41 into the boxes. Then have students track the details with the article on p. 40. Say: **First, the article tells how slime helps snails move. Then it tells how slime keeps the snail safe from harm. Then it tells how slime protects the snail in winter.** Point to the sentences on the board to show how the summary gives the details in the same order.

3. Read aloud the directions for Activity A on p. 43. Conduct the activity with the class. Discuss the logical order for the details. Point out that the order may vary.

4. Have students complete Activity B independently.

➤ **Extend the Lesson:** Have students label the topic sentence, details, and ending in other simple summaries.

Lesson 4 Reviewing a Summary

1. Review the qualities of a good summary: a topic sentence that names the writing being summarized, detail sentences that retell information, and an ending. Remind students that writers, when writing summaries, retell ideas and do not make up new details.

2. Read aloud "You Can't Find Me!" on p. 44 as students follow along. Check comprehension by asking questions such as: **Which animals eat an octopus?**

3. Ask a volunteer to read the summary on p. 45. Guide students through revising the draft. Ask: **Does the topic sentence tell what the article is about?** (yes) Point out that the second sentence is the same as the sentence in the article. Say: **This sentence gives a detail. Instead, it should summarize the idea that an octopus changes the way it looks.** Help students retell the idea in their own words. Ask: **Are the details in order?** (no) Guide students to put the sentences in order and to add a concluding sentence.

4. Have students write their revisions on a separate sheet of paper. Invite them to read aloud their summaries.

Page 43 / Student Book Page 28

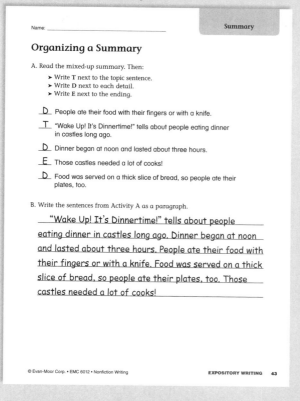

Pp. 44–45 and Sample Revision / Student Book pp. 29–30

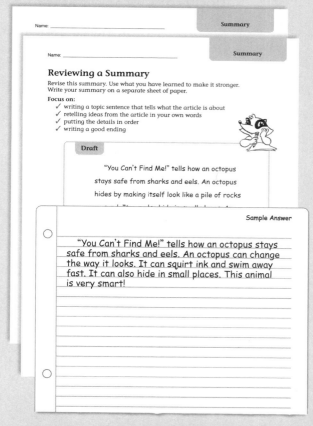

Name: _____

Introducing a Summary

Read this article about snails.

Snails and Slime

A snail has a soft body and no legs. This means it is hard for a snail to move around. So a snail makes a layer of slime under its body. Slime is very important to snails.

Slime makes it easier for snails to move from place to place. It is strong and sticky. Slime helps snails stick to leaves or walls.

Slime keeps a snail from getting hurt as it moves. It lets a snail move across rough stones. Slime even lets a snail move across sharp glass without getting hurt.

Slime also keeps snails safe during winter. A snail can pull its body into its shell to stay warm. It covers the shell's opening with slime. The slime turns hard and keeps out the cold air.

People may think slime is yucky. But for snails, slime is great!

Introducing a Summary

Read this example of a summary.

Writing Model

> "Snails and Slime" tells how slime helps snails.
> Snails use slime to move around. Slime helps snails
> stick to things. It keeps a snail safe from rough or
> sharp objects. Slime also keeps a snail safe inside
> its shell in winter. Slime is good for snails.

Writer's Purpose: _____

_____

Retelling in Your Own Words

Read each full sentence. Then use the sentence starter to write it a different way.

1. A sailboat uses the wind to go.

   The wind _____.

2. Black bears have short claws that help them climb trees.

   Black bears can climb trees because _____.

3. The cats chewed open their bag of treats and gobbled the crunchy fish inside.

   The cats _____.

4. Ginger kicked the soccer ball and scored a goal.

   Ginger _____.

5. Although penguins cannot fly, their wings are good for swimming.

   Penguins use their wings _____.

6. A cowboy hat keeps the sun out of your eyes and the rain off your face.

   A cowboy hat is a good hat to wear when _____.

You can say that again!

Name: _____

Organizing a Summary

A. Read the mixed-up summary. Then:

> ➤ Write **T** next to the topic sentence.
> ➤ Write **D** next to each detail.
> ➤ Write **E** next to the ending.

_____ People ate their food with their fingers or with a knife.

_____ "Wake Up! It's Dinnertime!" tells about people eating dinner in castles long ago.

_____ Dinner began at noon and lasted about three hours.

_____ Those castles needed a lot of cooks!

_____ Food was served on a thick slice of bread, so people ate their plates, too.

B. Write the sentences from Activity A as a paragraph.

_____

_____

_____

_____

_____

Reviewing a Summary

Read this article about an octopus.

You Can't Find Me!

An octopus might look like a blob with eight arms. But this sea animal is a yummy treat for sharks and eels. So an octopus must use many tricks to hide and stay safe.

An octopus hides by making itself look like a pile of rocks or sand. An octopus can change its skin color to brown, black, gray, or orange. It also can make its skin look bumpy like a rock. Or it can make its skin look smooth like fine sand. It is hard for sharks and eels to find a hiding octopus.

An octopus uses ink to stay safe. If a shark or an eel comes too close, the octopus squirts ink. The ink makes the water dark, so the shark or eel cannot see. Then the octopus swims away.

Small spaces are good hiding places for an octopus. The animal's body is soft, so it can push itself between rocks or into little holes. Sharks and eels are too big to follow the octopus.

The octopus is a clever animal! It can keep itself safe from enemies that are much bigger.

Reviewing a Summary

Revise this summary. Use what you have learned to make it stronger.
Write your summary on a separate sheet of paper.

Focus on:

✓ writing a topic sentence that tells what the article is about
✓ retelling ideas from the article in your own words
✓ putting the details in order
✓ writing a good ending

Draft

"You Can't Find Me!" tells how an octopus stays safe from sharks and eels. An octopus hides by making itself look like a pile of rocks or sand. It can also hide in small places. An octopus uses ink to stay safe.

Writing a Descriptive Paragraph

Page 49 / Student Book Page 32

Name: _____

Descriptive Paragraph

Introducing a Descriptive Paragraph
Read this example of a descriptive paragraph.

Writing Model

Barn Owls

Barn owls are interesting animals. They look different from other owls. They have creamy white faces shaped like a heart. Their bodies are small, but their wings stretch wide. Their long legs end in sharp claws. Barn owls do not hoot like other owls. They screech when they are angry. They also click their beaks to scare away enemies. But when they fly, they do not make a sound! Barn owls do not look or sound like other owls. But that is what makes them special.

Writer's Purpose: to describe barn owls _____

© Evan-Moor Corp. • EMC 6012 • Nonfiction Writing   **EXPOSITORY WRITING**   49

Page 50 / Student Book Page 33

Name: _____

Descriptive Paragraph

Writing a Topic Sentence

A. Each paragraph has a missing topic sentence. Read the paragraph. Then check the box next to the best topic sentence to begin the paragraph.

1. _____ The bark on some trees is rough and bumpy. The bark on other trees is smooth. Some trees have bark that peels off in thin strips.
   - ☐ All trees need trunks.
   - ☑ Not all tree bark feels the same.

2. _____ A happy dog wags its tail. A scared dog tucks its tail between its legs. A dog that is upset may growl.
   - ☑ Dogs show people how they feel.
   - ☐ Dogs are the best pets to have.

3. _____ The wind howled through the trees. Thunder boomed. Rain pounded the windows and the roof.
   - ☐ Wind can be very noisy.
   - ☑ The rainstorm made scary sounds.

B. Read each paragraph. Rewrite the underlined sentence so it tells what the paragraph is about.

1. There are many rides at the fair. The popcorn smells buttery. The cotton candy smells sweet. And the chicken wings smell spicy.

   Fair foods smell yummy.

2. Sea lions live in the ocean. Skin grows over their toes to form smooth flippers. A sea lion has three toenails. But you cannot really see a sea lion's toes.

   Sea lions have strange toes.

3. Tacos are easy to make. The meat is warm and juicy. The lettuce is crunchy. And the salsa is cool and spicy at the same time.

   Tacos are tasty.

50   **EXPOSITORY WRITING**   Nonfiction Writing • EMC 6012 • © Evan-Moor Corp.

Lesson 1 Introducing a Descriptive Paragraph

A descriptive paragraph describes a person, place, thing, or event, using vivid details, so readers can easily imagine that thing.

1. Ask students to think of a special place they have visited and to think about how they might describe that place to someone who has never been there. Explain that good, specific details help readers experience what the writer is describing.

2. Display "Barn Owls" on p. 49 and read it aloud as students follow along.

3. Ask: **What is the purpose of this descriptive paragraph?** (to describe barn owls) Have students write the purpose on the lines provided.

4. Invite students to offer opinions about what makes this a good descriptive paragraph. Prompt students by asking: **Does the writer tell what barn owls look like and sound like? Does the writer use words that help you imagine the owls? Can you imagine where the barn owls live?**

5. Explain that students will use the model as they study the skills needed to write a good descriptive paragraph.

➤ **Extend the Lesson:** Read aloud a description from a nonfiction text. Have students draw what they imagined as they listened to the description.

Lesson 2 Writing a Topic Sentence

1. Introduce topic sentences for a descriptive paragraph. Say: **A descriptive paragraph should begin with a topic sentence—a sentence that tells what the paragraph is going to describe.**

2. Read aloud the first sentence of the writing model and ask: **What is this paragraph going to describe?** (barn owls) Point out that this is the topic sentence of the paragraph.

3. Read aloud the directions for Activity A on p. 50. Read item 1 and model by saying: **The first possibility is "All trees need trunks." The paragraph doesn't mention trunks, so this probably is not a good topic sentence. All of the sentences in the paragraph are about different kinds of tree bark, so the second option is better.** Have students complete the activity independently or in pairs and review the answers as a class.

4. Direct students to Activity B. Read item 1 aloud and clarify that the underlined sentence is supposed to be the topic sentence. Ask: **Does this sentence tell about the paragraph?** (no) **What do the other sentences tell about?** (the smell of different foods at the fair) Guide students in writing a topic sentence for the paragraph. Explain that there are many ways to rewrite the topic sentence. Have students complete the activity in small groups. Invite volunteers to share their sentences. Discuss how each topic sentence tells about the other sentences in the paragraph.

➤ **Extend the Lesson:** Provide descriptive paragraphs from textbooks or released state tests. Have students find the topic sentence in each paragraph.

Lesson 3 Adding Sensory Details

1. Review the purpose of a descriptive paragraph.

2. Review the five senses. Explain: **Writers use sensory details, or details that tell about the senses, to help readers imagine what is being described.**

3. Guide students in finding details in "Barn Owls" that tell how these birds look and sound. (creamy white faces, small bodies, screech, do not make a sound when they fly, etc.)

4. Direct students to p. 51 and read aloud the directions. Model by completing the first item. Guide students to think of visual details. Then have students complete the activity independently or in small groups. Invite volunteers to share their answers.

➤ **Extend the Lesson:** Use sensory details to describe something in the classroom without telling what it is. (e.g., a rug: *red, fluffy, soft, round*) Then have partners take turns describing classroom objects and guessing them.

Lesson 4 Showing, Not Telling

1. Review the purpose of a descriptive paragraph.

2. Say: **Instead of telling your readers something, you can *show* them.** Write this sentence on the board: *Kim is funny.* Say: **This sentence just *tells* us that Kim is funny.** Then write this sentence on the board: *Kim's joke made Raina laugh out loud.* Say: **This sentence shows us that Kim is funny. We can imagine her telling a joke to someone.** Ask: **How else could you show that someone is funny?** (describe silly clothes the person wears or a gesture the person makes)

Page 51 / Student Book Page 34

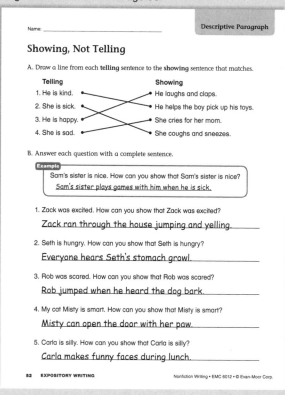

© Evan-Moor Corp. • EMC 6012 • Nonfiction Writing

Page 53 / Student Book Page 36

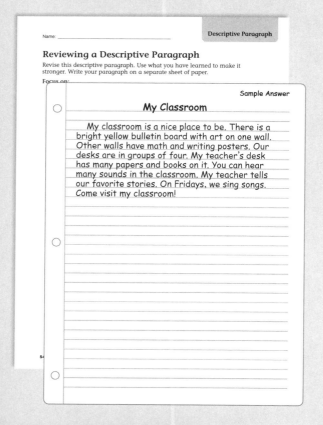

Page 54 and Sample Revision / Student Book Page 37

3. Direct students to Activity A on p. 52 and have them complete it in pairs. Review the answers together and discuss how the "showing" sentences are more descriptive.

4. Direct students to Activity B and read the example. Say: **The response explains what Sam's sister does that makes her seem nice.** Have students complete the activity in pairs or small groups. Ask volunteers to share their sentences.

Lesson 5 Expanding Sentences

1. Say: **Longer sentences can give more details for readers to picture. This can make the sentences more interesting.**

2. Write this sentence on the board and read it aloud: *Barn owls have white faces.* Say: **This sentence describes barn owls, but it doesn't give clear details.** Then read this sentence from "Barn Owls": *They have creamy white faces shaped like a heart.* Say: **This sentence gives us details to help us picture barn owls.**

3. Direct students to p. 53 and discuss the example. Point out that the expanded sentence gives clear details about where the bees were buzzing. Draw attention to the underlined word or words in each sentence. Say: **Make *that* detail clearer.** Expand the first item as a class. Then have students complete the activity in pairs.

➤ **Extend the Lesson:** Have students practice expanding sentences that they have written.

Lesson 6 Reviewing a Descriptive Paragraph

1. Review the qualities of a good descriptive paragraph: a topic sentence, sensory details, sentences that show rather than tell, and expanded sentences that provide more information.

2. Read aloud "My Classroom" on p. 54 as students follow along. Guide them through revising the draft. Ask: **Does the first sentence tell what the paragraph describes?** (yes) Read this sentence: *My teacher's desk is big.* Ask: **How might you change this sentence so it *shows* instead of *tells*?** (e.g., describe what the desk has on it) Say: **Look around our classroom to get ideas for details you might add.** Using students' suggestions, add details as a class.

3. Have students write their revisions on a separate sheet of paper. Invite volunteers to read aloud their revised descriptive paragraphs.

Introducing a Descriptive Paragraph

Read this example of a descriptive paragraph.

Writing Model

Barn Owls

Barn owls are interesting animals. They look different from other owls. They have creamy white faces shaped like a heart. Their bodies are small, but their wings stretch wide. Their long legs end in sharp claws. Barn owls do not hoot like other owls. They screech when they are angry. They also click their beaks to scare away enemies. But when they fly, they do not make a sound! Barn owls do not look or sound like other owls. But that is what makes them special.

Writer's Purpose: _____

_____

Name: _____

Writing a Topic Sentence

A. Each paragraph has a missing topic sentence. Read the paragraph. Then check the box next to the best topic sentence to begin the paragraph.

1. _____ The bark on some trees is rough and bumpy. The bark on other trees is smooth. Some trees have bark that peels off in thin strips.

   ☐ All trees need trunks.

   ☐ Not all tree bark feels the same.

2. _____ A happy dog wags its tail. A scared dog tucks its tail between its legs. A dog that is upset may growl.

   ☐ Dogs show people how they feel.

   ☐ Dogs are the best pets to have.

3. _____ The wind howled through the trees. Thunder boomed. Rain pounded the windows and the roof.

   ☐ Wind can be very noisy.

   ☐ The rainstorm made scary sounds.

B. Read each paragraph. Rewrite the underlined sentence so it tells what the paragraph is about.

1. There are many rides at the fair. The popcorn smells buttery. The cotton candy smells sweet. And the chicken wings smell spicy.

   _____

2. Sea lions live in the ocean. Skin grows over their toes to form smooth flippers. A sea lion has three toenails. But you cannot really see a sea lion's toes.

   _____

3. Tacos are easy to make. The meat is warm and juicy. The lettuce is crunchy. And the salsa is cool and spicy at the same time.

   _____

Adding Sensory Details

Complete each sentence. Then add details that describe the topic.

1. My favorite animal to look at is _____.

_____

_____

2. My favorite thing to smell is _____.

_____

_____

3. My favorite food to taste is _____.

_____

_____

4. My favorite stuffed animal to touch is _____.

_____

_____

5. My favorite sound to hear is _____.

_____

_____

Showing, Not Telling

A. Draw a line from each **telling** sentence to the **showing** sentence that matches.

Telling	**Showing**
1. He is kind. •	• He laughs and claps.
2. She is sick. •	• He helps the boy pick up his toys.
3. He is happy. •	• She cries for her mom.
4. She is sad. •	• She coughs and sneezes.

B. Answer each question with a complete sentence.

Example

Sam's sister is nice. How can you show that Sam's sister is nice?

Sam's sister plays games with him when he is sick.

1. Zack was excited. How can you show that Zack was excited?

_____

2. Seth is hungry. How can you show that Seth is hungry?

_____

3. Rob was scared. How can you show that Rob was scared?

_____

4. My cat Misty is smart. How can you show that Misty is smart?

_____

5. Carla is silly. How can you show that Carla is silly?

_____

Expanding Sentences

Rewrite each sentence to make it more descriptive.

> The bees were <u>buzzing</u>.
>
> <u>The bees were buzzing in the tall yellow sunflowers.</u>

1. I heard dogs <u>barking</u>.

_____

2. Snow <u>fell</u>.

_____

3. The trumpet <u>played</u>.

_____

4. Everyone ate the <u>meal</u>.

_____

5. A <u>lizard</u> slithered into the garden.

_____

6. The rocket <u>zoomed</u>.

_____

7. The butterfly <u>flew away</u>.

_____

Reviewing a Descriptive Paragraph

Revise this descriptive paragraph. Use what you have learned to make it stronger. Write your paragraph on a separate sheet of paper.

Focus on:

✓ writing a topic sentence that tells what you are describing

✓ using details that tell how something looks, feels, sounds, smells, or tastes

✓ writing sentences that "show" rather than "tell"

Draft

My Classroom

My classroom is a nice place to be. There is a bulletin board on one wall. Other walls have posters. Our desks are in groups. My teacher's desk is big. You can hear many sounds in the classroom. My teacher tells stories. We sing. Come visit my classroom!

Writing a Biography

Lesson 1 Introducing a Biography

A biography tells important information about a person's life.

1. Tell students that a biography is a type of writing that gives important information about someone's life, including when and where the person was born, what events were significant in that person's life, and what accomplishments the person is known for.

2. Read aloud "The Woman Who Knows Chimps" on p. 58 as students follow along. Clarify that *expert* means someone who knows a lot about a subject and that *chimp* is short for *chimpanzee*.

3. Ask: **What is the purpose of this biography?** (to tell about the life of Jane Goodall) Have students write the purpose on the lines provided.

4. Invite students to offer opinions about what makes this a good biography. Prompt students by asking: **Does the first sentence tell whom the biography is about? Does the biography tell when she was born? Does it include interesting facts about her? Are the facts in the order in which they happened?**

5. Explain that students will use the model as they study the skills needed to write a good biography.

➤ **Extend the Lesson:** As a class, brainstorm subjects for a biography. Generate a list of people who students may want to write about, including people who are familiar but not famous (e.g., parents).

Lesson 2 Gathering Facts

1. Remind students that a biography includes when and where a person was born, important things that person has done, and what that person is known for.

2. Say: **A good biography tells facts that are important to know about a person.** Review the model on p. 58. Ask: **Whom is this biography about?** (Jane Goodall) **Where and when was she born?** (England, 1934) **What is she best known for?** (being an expert on chimpanzees) Guide students to identify other facts.

3. Ask: **How do you suppose writers find out facts that they can include in a biography?** Think aloud with students and guide their responses. Then say: **One way to find out a fact about someone's life is to ask him or her a question.**

Page 58 / Student Book Page 39

Name: _____

Biography

Introducing a Biography
Read this example of a biography.

Writing Model

The Woman Who Knows Chimps

Jane Goodall is an expert on chimpanzees, which are a kind of ape. Jane was born in England in 1934. When she was only a year old, her father gave her a stuffed toy chimp. She loved it! She wanted to study wild animals when she grew up. In 1960, Jane went to Africa to study wild chimps. She stayed there for 25 years. She learned many things about chimps that no one knew before. Today, Dr. Jane Goodall travels all over the world. She speaks about animal rights and about making the world a better place.

Writer's Purpose: to tell about the life of Jane Goodall

_____

58   EXPOSITORY WRITING   Nonfiction Writing • EMC 6012 • © Evan-Moor Corp.

Page 59 / Student Book Page 40

Name: _____

Biography

Gathering Facts

Talk to a partner. Find out the answer to each question. Then write it as a complete sentence.

Examples

What is your partner's name?
My partner's name is Zari Daniels.

What makes your partner special?
She wants to be an astronaut.

1. What is your partner's name?
My partner's name is Roberto Mendes.

2. When was your partner born?
Roberto was born in 2004.

3. Where was your partner born?
He was born in Lubbock, Texas.

4. What is your partner's favorite thing to do?
He likes to go fishing.

5. What is the most important thing that ever happened to your partner?
He won a pie-eating contest.

6. What makes your partner special?
He knows how to tie many kinds of knots.

© Evan-Moor Corp. • EMC 6012 • Nonfiction Writing   **EXPOSITORY WRITING**   59

Page 60 / Student Book Page 41

Name: _____

Biography

Writing a Topic Sentence

A. Each paragraph has a missing topic sentence. Read the paragraph. Then check the box next to the best topic sentence to begin the biography.

1. _____ Like Jane Goodall, she loved animals. She studied wild gorillas in the mountains of Africa. She watched the gorillas to find out how they lived.
   ☐ Dian Fossey was friends with Jane Goodall.
   ☑ Dian Fossey was a gorilla expert.

2. _____ He writes books for children. He draws pictures for his books, too. Children everywhere know Eric Carle's book *The Very Hungry Caterpillar.*
   ☑ Eric Carle is a famous writer and artist.
   ☐ Eric Carle loves nature.

3. _____ As a child, he learned to play the piano. He played with many groups before forming his own band. His band had a beat all its own!
   ☑ Count Basie was a jazz bandleader.
   ☐ Count Basie's real name was William Basie.

B. Complete each topic sentence so it tells about the person.

1. Dr. Cheryl Cullion is _a zoo animal doctor_. She keeps the zoo animals healthy. She can help a giraffe in pain. And she can trick a penguin into taking its medicine!

2. Stephen Hillenburg created _a TV series for kids_. First he studied ocean science. Then he went to art school. He made a cartoon about a sponge. That is how *SpongeBob SquarePants* was born!

3. Amelia Earhart was _an airplane pilot_. She learned to fly in 1921. Soon after, she bought her own airplane. It was bright yellow, and she named it Canary. Amelia set many records as a pilot.

60   **EXPOSITORY WRITING**   Nonfiction Writing • EMC 6012 • © Evan-Moor Corp.

---

4. Read the directions for the activity on p. 59. Then read the examples and discuss other things that make someone special. (e.g., a unique trait such as curly red hair, a special talent or skill, an interesting family) Ask: **What are some different ways to answer the questions using complete sentences?** (use the person's name, use *he* or *she*, write *My partner*) Then have students complete the activity in pairs. Invite volunteers to share one or two of their sentences with the class.

➤ **Extend the Lesson:** As a class, brainstorm other questions a writer might find answers to while gathering facts for a biography. (e.g., where the person went to school, facts about the person's family, what the person had dreamed of doing when he or she became an adult)

Lesson 3 Writing a Topic Sentence

1. Review the purpose of a biography. Then review the concept of a topic sentence. Say: **In a biography, the topic sentence tells whom the biography is about and what the person is known for. The topic sentence is often the first sentence in the paragraph.**

2. Have students underline the topic sentence in the writing model on p. 58. Say: **This sentence tells who Jane Goodall is and what she is best known for.** Suggest other ways to phrase the main idea. (e.g., The scientist Jane Goodall is best known for her research on chimpanzees.)

3. Model Activity A on p. 60, using item 1. Ask: **Are the sentences in this paragraph mostly about studying gorillas, or are they about Dian Fossey's friendship with Jane Goodall?** (studying gorillas) Say: **The sentence "Dian Fossey was a gorilla expert" is a better topic sentence.** Then have students complete the activity in pairs.

4. Model Activity B, using item 1. Say: **This short biography is about Dr. Cheryl Cullion. The "Dr." in front of her name means she is a doctor. The sentences say that she cares for giraffes, penguins, and other animals at the zoo. Her job is to keep the animals healthy. The main idea is that Cheryl Cullion is an animal doctor who works at the zoo. The topic sentence should say that.** Have students work independently or in pairs to complete items 2 and 3. Remind students to look for clues in the paragraph to determine how to complete the topic sentence.

Lesson 4 Organizing a Biography

1. Review the purpose of a biography.

2. Say: **Because a biography tells about a person's life, the facts are organized in time order, or the order in which they happened.**

3. Draw a timeline on the board and label it "Jane Goodall's Life." Remind students that a timeline shows events in time order. Have students identify the main events from "The Woman Who Knows Chimps." Record them on the timeline and point out that they are presented in time order. Ask: **What clues tell us the order of the events?** (dates, age, time words such as *today*)

4. Direct students to p. 61. Read aloud the captions in the timeline for Dr. Helen Greiner (GRAY-nur). Ask volunteers to read the topic sentence and the concluding sentence below the timeline. Then model forming a sentence based on the first timeline label. (e.g., Helen was born in England in 1967.) Have students complete the activity independently or in small groups. Invite volunteers to read aloud their biographies.

➤ **Extend the Lesson:** Have students make timelines of their own lives, noting events that they consider important.

Lesson 5 Reviewing a Biography

1. Review the qualities of a good biography: a topic sentence that identifies the person and tells what he or she is known for; important facts about the person, including when he or she was born; and other facts about the person, organized in time order.

2. Ask students who have read or heard of the Jigsaw Jones mystery books to share what they know. Help students gather facts about the author, James Preller, from book jackets or the Internet.

3. Read aloud "James and Jigsaw" on p. 62 as students follow along. Then guide students through revising the draft. Ask: **Does the first sentence tell who the biography is about?** (yes) **Does it tell what he is known for?** (no) **What information should the topic sentence include?** (that James Preller is a well-known author) **Does the paragraph organize the facts in time order?** (no) **Which fact should come near the beginning?** (that he was born in 1961)

4. Have students write their revisions on a separate sheet of paper. Invite volunteers to share their revisions.

Page 61 / Student Book Page 42

Name: _____   Biography

Organizing a Biography

Read the timeline. Then fill in the paragraph below to tell about Dr. Helen Greiner's life. The topic sentence and the concluding sentence have been written for you.

Timeline of Dr. Helen Greiner's Life

1967	1985	1991	2002
Helen was born in England.	Helen went to college to study computer science.	Helen started a company to make robots.	Helen helped build a robot that cleans floors.

Dr. Helen Greiner makes robots that work for people. Helen was born in England in 1967. She went to college in 1985 to study computer science. In 1991, she started a company to make robots. In 2002, she helped build a robot that cleans floors.

Helen wants to change the world with robots.

EXPOSITORY WRITING 61

Page 62 and Sample Revision/ Student Book Page 43

Name: _____   Biography

Reviewing a Biography

Revise this biography. Use what you have learned to make it stronger. Write the biography on a separate sheet of paper.

Sample Answer

James and Jigsaw

    James Preller is a famous author. He writes the Jigsaw Jones mystery books for kids. James was born in 1961 in New York. He wrote his first children's book in 1986. Since then, he has written more than 30 books about Jigsaw. Today, James is writing new books for kids.

Name: _____

Introducing a Biography

Read this example of a biography.

The Woman Who Knows Chimps

Jane Goodall is an expert on chimpanzees, which are a kind of ape. Jane was born in England in 1934. When she was only a year old, her father gave her a stuffed toy chimp. She loved it! She wanted to study wild animals when she grew up. In 1960, Jane went to Africa to study wild chimps. She stayed there for 25 years. She learned many things about chimps that no one knew before. Today, Dr. Jane Goodall travels all over the world. She speaks about animal rights and about making the world a better place.

Writer's Purpose: _____

_____

Gathering Facts

Talk to a partner. Find out the answer to each question. Then write it as a complete sentence.

Examples

What is your partner's name?

<u>My partner's name is Zari Daniels.</u>

What makes your partner special?

<u>She wants to be an astronaut.</u>

1. What is your partner's name?

_____

2. When was your partner born?

_____

3. Where was your partner born?

_____

4. What is your partner's favorite thing to do?

_____

5. What is the most important thing that ever happened to your partner?

_____

6. What makes your partner special?

_____

Name: _____

Writing a Topic Sentence

A. Each paragraph has a missing topic sentence. Read the paragraph. Then check the box next to the best topic sentence to begin the biography.

1. _____ Like Jane Goodall, she loved animals. She studied wild gorillas in the mountains of Africa. She watched the gorillas to find out how they lived.

   ☐ Dian Fossey was friends with Jane Goodall.

   ☐ Dian Fossey was a gorilla expert.

2. _____ He writes books for children. He draws pictures for his books, too. Children everywhere know Eric Carle's book *The Very Hungry Caterpillar.*

   ☐ Eric Carle is a famous writer and artist.

   ☐ Eric Carle loves nature.

3. _____ As a child, he learned to play the piano. He played with many groups before forming his own band. His band had a beat all its own!

   ☐ Count Basie was a jazz bandleader.

   ☐ Count Basie's real name was William Basie.

B. Complete each topic sentence so it tells about the person.

1. Dr. Cheryl Cullion is _____. She keeps the zoo animals healthy. She can help a giraffe in pain. And she can trick a penguin into taking its medicine!

2. Stephen Hillenburg created _____. First he studied ocean science. Then he went to art school. He made a cartoon about a sponge. That is how *SpongeBob SquarePants* was born!

3. Amelia Earhart was _____. She learned to fly in 1921. Soon after, she bought her own airplane. It was bright yellow, and she named it Canary. Amelia set many records as a pilot.

Organizing a Biography

Read the timeline. Then fill in the paragraph below to tell about Dr. Helen Greiner's life. The topic sentence and the concluding sentence have been written for you.

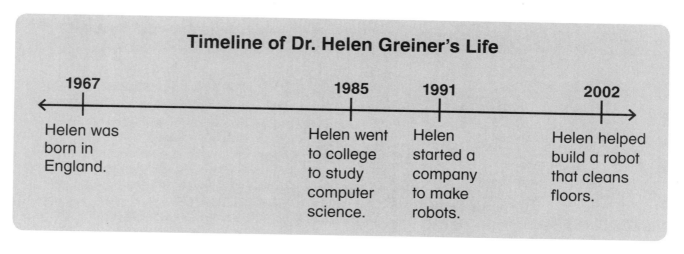

Dr. Helen Greiner makes robots that work for people. _____

_____

_____

_____

_____

Helen wants to change the world with robots.

Name: _____

Reviewing a Biography

Revise this biography. Use what you have learned to make it stronger. Write the biography on a separate sheet of paper.

Focus on:

✓ writing a topic sentence that tells whom the biography is about
✓ giving details about the person in time order
✓ using dates and clue words to show the order of events

Draft

James and Jigsaw

James Preller wrote his first children's book in 1986. He writes mystery books about a character named Jigsaw Jones. He has written more than 30 books about Jigsaw. James was born in 1961 in New York. Today, James is writing new books for kids.

Nonfiction Writing • EMC 6012 • © Evan-Moor Corp.

Writing Directions

Lesson 1 Introducing Directions

Directions tell the reader how to make or do something.

1. Tell students that when they want to explain in writing how to make something, such as a birdhouse, or how to do something, such as take care of a pet, they can write a set of directions.

2. Read aloud "Frozen Treats" on p. 66 as students follow along. Encourage students to visualize each step.

3. Ask: **What is the purpose of these directions?** (to tell how to make frozen treats) Have students write the purpose on the lines provided.

4. Invite students to offer opinions about what makes this a good set of directions. Prompt students by asking: **Does the first sentence explain what the directions are for? Does the next sentence tell what materials you would need? Are the directions clear and easy to follow? Are the steps in order from first to last?**

5. Explain that students will use the model as they study the skills needed to write how-to directions.

➤ **Extend the Lesson:** Tell students that directions are often presented as bulleted or numbered lists, with separate materials lists and sometimes pictures or diagrams. Display simple recipes and articles with step-by-step instructions from online or print magazines for students.

Lesson 2 Writing an Introduction

1. Review the purpose of directions.

2. Say: **It's important when writing directions that you first tell people what they will be making or doing, and what materials they will need. Writers give this information in the introduction, or the first couple of sentences of the paragraph.** Read aloud the first sentence of the model on p. 66 and point out that it's the topic sentence. Ask: **What do these directions explain how to do?** (make frozen juice pops) Read the second sentence and ask: **What materials will readers need in order to make the juice pops?** (small paper cups, juice, foil, and craft sticks)

3. Read the directions for Activity A on p. 67. Then read the first topic and ask: **What materials would you need in order to make a kite?** Clarify that students will write the number of the topic next to the set of materials. Then have students complete the activity in pairs.

Page 66 / Student Book Page 45

Name: _____

Directions

Introducing Directions
Read this example of directions.

Writing Model

Frozen Treats

You can make your own frozen juice pops. All you need are small paper cups, juice, foil, and craft sticks. First, pour the juice into each small cup. Next, cover the top of each cup with foil. Then push a craft stick through the center of the foil. Put the cups into the freezer for 8 hours. Frozen treats are cool on a hot summer day.

Writer's Purpose: to tell how to make frozen treats _____

66 EXPOSITORY WRITING   Nonfiction Writing • EMC 6012 • © Evan-Moor Corp.

Page 67 / Student Book Page 46

Name: _____

Directions

Writing an Introduction

A. Write the number of each topic next to the materials that go with that topic.

Topic	Materials
1. how to make a kite	_5_ plates, forks, spoons
2. how to clean your room	_1_ wooden rods, paper, string
3. how to shape a clay bowl	_4_ cage, bedding, food dish
4. how to care for a pet rabbit	_6_ game board, game pieces
5. how to set the table	_2_ broom, dustpan, dust cloth
6. how to play checkers	_3_ clay

B. Choose three topics from above. For each topic, write an introduction for a set of directions.

Example

Topic: how to make a kite
It is easy to make a kite. You need wooden rods, paper, and string.

1. Here is a good way to clean your room. You will need a broom, a dustpan, and a dust cloth.

2. It is fun to shape a bowl from clay. It only takes some clay and a little skill.

3. Anyone can care for a pet rabbit. You just need a cage, some bedding, and a food dish.

© Evan-Moor Corp. • EMC 6012 • Nonfiction Writing   **EXPOSITORY WRITING** 67

---

4. Read the directions and the example for Activity B. Remind students that the topic sentence should identify what readers will learn to make or do. Point out that there are many ways to introduce the topic. Say: **You could tell how many steps the activity involves or how often the task needs to be done. Or you could tell about the topic by saying that it's fun or easy or difficult to do.** Remind students that the introduction also lists the materials that readers will need. Suggest that they use the Activity A lists, but encourage them to be creative, too. Have students complete the activity independently or in pairs.

➤ **Extend the Lesson:** Have students practice writing introductions (a topic sentence and a sentence listing materials) for popular games such as hide-and-seek.

Lesson 3 Making It Clear

1. Demonstrate the importance of clear instructions by saying: **Take out a sheet of paper and fold it.** Then invite students to display their folded papers. Say: **Some of your papers are folded differently because the direction I gave was not clear.** Ask: **What if I said to take out a sheet of drawing paper and fold it in half from top to bottom? Are those directions clearer?** (yes) Say: **Writers need to use clear and specific language so readers can follow the directions.**

2. Review "Frozen Treats" and ask: **Would you be able to follow these directions? What words make the steps clear in your mind?** Encourage comments.

3. Write these sentences on the board: *Put the cups into the freezer. Put the cups into the freezer for 8 hours.* Ask: **Which sentence is clearer?** (The second one) **Why is it clearer?** (It tells how long it takes for the juice to freeze.)

4. Read the directions and example for Activity A on p. 68. Point out the drawing of the mask. Explain: **The new sentence is clearer because it tells what kind of shape to cut from a piece of cardboard.** Remind students to refer to the mask drawing as they complete the activity.

5. Read Activity B. Ask: **Do the directions say where to pour the milk or how much syrup to add?** (no) Then have students complete the activity in pairs.

➤ **Extend the Lesson:** Have students write three or four clear steps for a popular game or an everyday activity.

Page 68 / Student Book Page 47

Name: _____

Directions

Making It Clear

A. The four steps below tell how to make an animal mask, but they are not very clear. Rewrite each step and make it clearer by answering the question.

Example
Cut out a shape from a piece of cardboard. (What kind of shape?)
Cut out a circle from a piece of cardboard.

1. Draw the face. (What parts of the face?)
Draw the eyes, nose, mouth, and hair.

2. Cut out two holes. (What are they for?)
Cut out two holes for the eyes.

3. Cut two long pieces of string. (How long?)
Cut two pieces of string about 10 inches long.

4. Put one piece of string on each side of the mask. (How?)
Staple one piece of string to each side of the mask.

B. Revise these directions for making chocolate milk. Make them clearer.

Pour some milk. Add some chocolate syrup. Then stir.
Pour milk into a glass. Add a spoonful of chocolate syrup to the milk. Stir until the syrup is mixed into the milk.

68 EXPOSITORY WRITING   Nonfiction Writing • EMC 6012 • © Evan-Moor Corp.

Lesson 4 Organizing Directions

1. Review the purpose of directions.

2. Say: **It is important to write the steps in the correct order. Otherwise, people can make a mistake when they follow the directions.** Review the writing model. Ask: **What is the first step in making frozen juice pops?** (pouring the juice into cups) **What is the last step?** (freezing the cups of juice)

3. Invite two students to demonstrate how to play tic-tac-toe. Discuss the steps involved in playing the game. Then read the directions for Activity A on p. 69. Invite volunteers to read aloud the sentences. Guide students to identify the topic sentence and the materials sentence and to number them 1 and 2. Then guide students to identify the ending sentence and number it 7. Have students complete the activity in pairs or small groups. Review the answers as a class.

4. Have students complete Activity B independently.

➤ **Extend the Lesson:** Explain that acting out the steps in a set of directions can help writers determine the sequence. Have students act out directions for distinctive activities, such as making a snowman or a sand castle.

Lesson 5 Reviewing Directions

1. Review the qualities of good how-to directions: an introduction that states the topic and lists the materials needed, clear instructions, and steps organized in the order they occur.

2. Read aloud "How to Wash a Car" on p. 70 as students follow along. Then guide students through revising the draft. Ask: **Does the first sentence tell what the directions are for?** (no) **Does the second sentence name all of the materials needed, based on the rest of the directions?** (No. It doesn't include a towel.) **Are any steps out of order?** (yes) **Which step is out of order?** (You need to close the windows before washing the car.) **Which steps could be clearer?** If students have trouble answering, ask: **Do any of the sentences tell you how to rinse off the soap?** (no) **What would make that step clearer?** (telling people to use the hose)

3. Have students write their directions on a separate sheet of paper. Invite volunteers to share their revisions.

Name: _____   Directions

Organizing Directions

A. Number the sentences to show the best order.

Tic-Tac-Toe

_2_ You just need a pencil and some paper.

_5_ Then player 2 takes a turn.

_7_ It is hard to win this game!

_1_ You can play tic-tac-toe anywhere.

_3_ First, draw a grid that has nine squares.

_4_ Next, player 1 writes an X or an O in one square.

_6_ The game continues, as players try to get three X's or O's together in a straight line.

B. Write the steps for playing tic-tac-toe. Use the sentences from above. Write them in the correct order.

Tic-Tac-Toe

You can play tic-tac-toe anywhere. You just need a pencil and some paper. First, draw a grid that has nine squares. Next, player 1 writes an X or an O in one square. Then player 2 takes a turn. The game continues, as players try to get three X's or O's together in a straight line. It is hard to win this game!

© Evan-Moor Corp. • EMC 6012 • Nonfiction Writing   **EXPOSITORY WRITING** 69

Name: _____   Directions

Reviewing Directions

Revise these directions. Use what you have learned to make them stronger. Write your directions on a separate sheet of paper.

Focus

Sample Answer

How to Wash a Car

You can have fun washing a car! You need a bucket, a hose, some soap, a sponge, and an old towel. First, close all of the car windows. Then rub the car with a wet, soapy sponge. Use the hose to rinse off the soap. Last, wipe the car dry with a towel.

70

Name: _____

Introducing Directions

Read this example of directions.

Writing Model

Frozen Treats

You can make your own frozen juice pops. All you need are small paper cups, juice, foil, and craft sticks. First, pour the juice into each small cup. Next, cover the top of each cup with foil. Then push a craft stick through the center of the foil. Put the cups into the freezer for 8 hours. Frozen treats are cool on a hot summer day.

Writer's Purpose: _____

_____

Nonfiction Writing • EMC 6012 • © Evan-Moor Corp.

Writing an Introduction

A. Write the number of each topic next to the materials that go with that topic.

Topic

1. how to make a kite
2. how to clean your room
3. how to shape a clay bowl
4. how to care for a pet rabbit
5. how to set the table
6. how to play checkers

Materials

_____ plates, forks, spoons

_____ wooden rods, paper, string

_____ cage, bedding, food dish

_____ game board, game pieces

_____ broom, dustpan, dust cloth

_____ clay

B. Choose three topics from above. For each topic, write an introduction for a set of directions.

Example

Topic: how to make a kite
It is easy to make a kite. You need wooden rods, paper, and string.

1. _____

_____

2. _____

_____

3. _____

_____

Name: _____

Making It Clear

A. The four steps below tell how to make an animal mask,
but they are not very clear. Rewrite each step and
make it clearer by answering the question.

Example

Cut out a shape from a piece of cardboard.
(What kind of shape?)
<u>Cut out a circle from a piece of cardboard.</u>

1. Draw the face. (What parts of the face?)

   _____

2. Cut out two holes. (What are they for?)

   _____

3. Cut two long pieces of string. (How long?)

   _____

4. Put one piece of string on each side of the mask. (How?)

   _____

B. Revise these directions for making chocolate milk. Make them clearer.

   Pour some milk. Add some chocolate syrup. Then stir.

   _____

   _____

   _____

Name: _____

Organizing Directions

A. Number the sentences to show the best order.

Tic-Tac-Toe

_____ You just need a pencil and some paper.

_____ Then player 2 takes a turn.

_____ It is hard to win this game!

_____ You can play tic-tac-toe anywhere.

_____ First, draw a grid that has nine squares.

_____ Next, player 1 writes an **X** or an **O** in one square.

_____ The game continues, as players try to get three X's or O's together in a straight line.

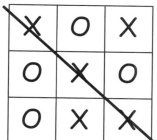

B. Write the steps for playing tic-tac-toe. Use the sentences from above. Write them in the correct order.

Tic-Tac-Toe

_____

_____

_____

_____

_____

_____

_____

EXPOSITORY WRITING

Reviewing Directions

Revise these directions. Use what you have learned to make them stronger.
Write your directions on a separate sheet of paper.

Focus on:

✓ writing a sentence that tells what the directions are for
✓ writing a sentence that tells what someone needs for the activity
✓ making the directions clear
✓ putting the steps in order

Draft

How to Wash a Car

You can have fun doing this! You need a
bucket, a hose, some soap, and a sponge.
First, rub the car with a sponge. Be sure
to close the windows. Rinse off the soap.
Last, dry it with a towel.

Writing a News Article

Lesson 1 Introducing a News Article

A news article is a type of writing that reports facts and information about an event that has just happened. It answers who, what, where, when, why, *and* how.

1. Display a newspaper article and say: **News articles tell about something that actually happened. The writer is usually called a** *reporter.* Point out the headline; beginning sentence, or lead; and other elements of the news article.

2. Read aloud "Second-Grade Gardeners" on p. 74 as students follow along. Encourage them to listen for the facts in the article.

3. Ask: **What is the purpose of this news article?** (to give some news about a school garden) Have students write the purpose on the lines provided.

4. Invite students to offer opinions about what makes this a good news article. Prompt students by asking: **Does the reporter tell you right away what happened? Does the reporter tell when, where, and why it happened and who was involved? Did the event just happen?**

5. Explain that students will use the model as they study the skills needed to write a good news article.

➤ **Extend the Lesson:** Invite students to suggest news items related to their own class (or school) that could be described in a news article (e.g., a recently acquired classroom pet, a recent field trip, or a school production).

Lesson 2 Finding the 5Ws and H

1. Review the purpose of a news article. Say: **A good news article tells most of the 5Ws and H: who, what, where, when, why, and how.**

2. Say: **Before a reporter can write a news article, he or she must gather the 5Ws and H.**

3. On the board, draw a graphic organizer that consists of a large circle with six smaller circles around it. Write *"Second-Grade Gardeners"* in the center circle. Label the other circles *Who, What, Where, When, Why,* and *How.* Review the model on p. 74 and ask: **What is the news event in this article?** (Students planted a garden.) Record the information in the *What* circle. Then ask: **Where did it happen?** (Murray School) **Why?** (The students wanted to grow food …) Continue filling in the graphic organizer as a class.

Page 74 / Student Book Page 51

Name: _____

News Article

Introducing a News Article
Read this example of a news article.

Writing Model

Second-Grade Gardeners

The students in Ms. Tucker's class planted seedlings last Monday for a vegetable garden at Murray School. They wanted to grow food for the school and learn about gardening, too. The students chose a sunny spot next to the back wall. Parents came to help. They dug holes in the soil. The students planted cabbage, radishes, carrots, and other vegetables. Ms. Tucker hopes the whole school will use the garden in the future.

Writer's Purpose: to give some news about a school garden

Nonfiction Writing • EMC 6012 • © Evan-Moor Corp.

© Evan-Moor Corp. • EMC 6012 • Nonfiction Writing

EXPOSITORY WRITING 71

Page 75 / Student Book Page 52

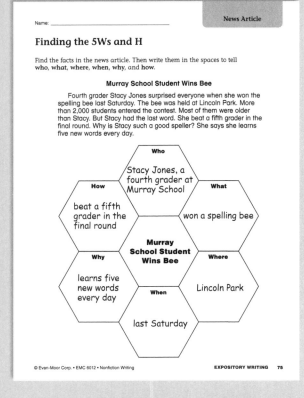

Page 76 / Student Book Page 53

4. Direct students to p. 75. Read aloud the news article "Murray School Student Wins Bee" as students follow along. Then ask: **What news does this article report?** (A fourth grader from Murray School won a spelling bee.) Tell students to record this information in the *What* cell of the graphic organizer. Then have students complete the graphic organizer in small groups. Review the answers as a class.

➤ **Extend the Lesson:** Have students work in small groups to complete a 5Ws-and-H web for an actual event at school, such as a food drive or picture day.

Lesson 3 Writing a Good Lead

1. Review the purpose of a news article.

2. Tell students that a good news article has a beginning sentence, or *lead*, that grabs readers' attention. **Say: A lead makes readers want to keep reading. It tells what the news is and answers at least one of the 5Ws and H.**

3. Read the lead in the model on p. 74: *The students in Ms. Tucker's class planted seedlings last Monday for a vegetable garden at Murray School.* Ask: **Why might this sentence make you want to read on?** (e.g., It sounds interesting; I want to find out what they planted.) Then ask: **Which of the 5Ws or H does it include?** (who, what, where, when, and why)

4. Read aloud the directions for Activity A on p. 76. Then read the first item. Ask: **Which sentence grabs your attention more? Why? Do both sentences tell about an event that happened?** (no) **Which one does?** *(Jim Blume became a hero last Monday.)* Have students complete the activity independently. Discuss the answers with the class.

5. Read aloud the directions for Activity B. Read the underlined sentences and discuss why they are not good leads. (They do not tell what happened.) Point out that there is more than one way to revise the lead. Then have students complete the activity in small groups. Invite volunteers to share their answers.

➤ **Extend the Lesson:** Have students work in pairs to write a lead about something that each of them did recently. (e.g., attended a birthday party, visited a relative in another town)

Lesson 4 Adding Details

1. Review the purpose of a news article. Say: **A good news article is interesting to read and uses complete sentences to give information.** You may want to have students identify the subject and predicate in two or three of the sentences in the writing model.

2. Explain that a sentence can express more than one fact. Reread the first sentence of the writing model and say: **This sentence tells who, what, when, *and* where the event occurred. It expresses four facts.**

3. Direct students to p. 77. Have two students take turns reading the reporter's notebook. Use the first item to model the activity. Say: **The details you add in this case should tell *who* and *where* the animals were.** Have students complete the activity in pairs or small groups. Then invite them to share their sentences with the class.

➤ **Extend the Lesson:** Have students write a news article based on the reporter's notes.

Lesson 5 Reviewing a News Article

1. Review the qualities of a good news article: a lead sentence that answers some of the 5Ws and H, and interesting details that answer more.

2. Make sure students know the story of Snow White. Summarize it if necessary. Read aloud "Snow White Is Alive!" on p. 78 as students follow along. Then guide students through revising the draft. Ask: **What news does this article report?** (The Prince woke up Snow White.) Help students identify the 5Ws and H in the article. Reread the first sentence and ask: **Does the lead tell what the news is?** (yes) Then read the second sentence and ask: **How can we change the beginning so the lead answers more of the 5Ws?** (combine the first two sentences) **What detail can we add that tells what Snow White looked like when she woke up?** (e.g., She was smiling.) Help students add details that explain why the seven dwarfs cheered. (e.g., They were happy that Snow White was still alive.) Help them add details to explain why the dwarfs had thought that Snow White was dead. (e.g., She had not moved since she had eaten last year.)

3. Have students write their news articles on a separate sheet of paper. Invite volunteers to share their revisions with the class.

Page 77 / Student Book Page 54

Name: _____   News Article

Adding Details

Read the reporter's notes about something that happened at a zoo. Then read each sentence below. Follow the directions to rewrite the sentence, using details from the notes.

Who?	monkeys
What happened?	they escaped
Where?	City Park Zoo
How?	climbed nearby trees
When?	Friday morning
Why?	they like to make trouble

1. A few animals escaped. (Tell **who** and **where**.)
   A few monkeys escaped from the City Park Zoo.

2. Some monkeys were able to get away. (Tell **how**.)
   Some monkeys were able to get away by climbing nearby trees.

3. The clever monkeys got out. (Tell **why**.)
   The clever monkeys got out because they like to make trouble.

4. Something terrible happened at the zoo. (Tell **what** and **when**.)
   Some monkeys escaped from the zoo on Friday morning.

© Evan-Moor Corp. • EMC 6012 • Nonfiction Writing   EXPOSITORY WRITING **77**

Page 78 and Sample Revision / Student Book Page 55

Name: _____   News Article

Reviewing a News Article

Revise this news article. Use what you have learned to make it stronger. Write the news article on a separate sheet of paper.

Sample Answer

Snow White Is Alive!

The Prince woke Snow White from a deep sleep yesterday. She stepped out of her glass box with a smile. The seven dwarfs cheered when they saw Snow White. They had thought their friend was dead, because she had eaten a poisoned apple last year and had not moved since then. The Prince's kiss woke her. The Prince and Snow White plan to get married next spring.

Introducing a News Article

Read this example of a news article.

Writing Model

Second-Grade Gardeners

The students in Ms. Tucker's class planted seedlings last Monday for a vegetable garden at Murray School. They wanted to grow food for the school and learn about gardening, too. The students chose a sunny spot next to the back wall. Parents came to help. They dug holes in the soil. The students planted cabbage, radishes, carrots, and other vegetables. Ms. Tucker hopes the whole school will use the garden in the future.

Writer's Purpose: _____

_____

Finding the 5Ws and H

Find the facts in the news article. Then write them in the spaces to tell
who, what, where, when, why, and **how.**

Murray School Student Wins Bee

Fourth grader Stacy Jones surprised everyone when she won the
spelling bee last Saturday. The bee was held at Lincoln Park. More
than 2,000 students entered the contest. Most of them were older
than Stacy. But Stacy had the last word. She beat a fifth grader in the
final round. Why is Stacy such a good speller? She says she learns
five new words every day.

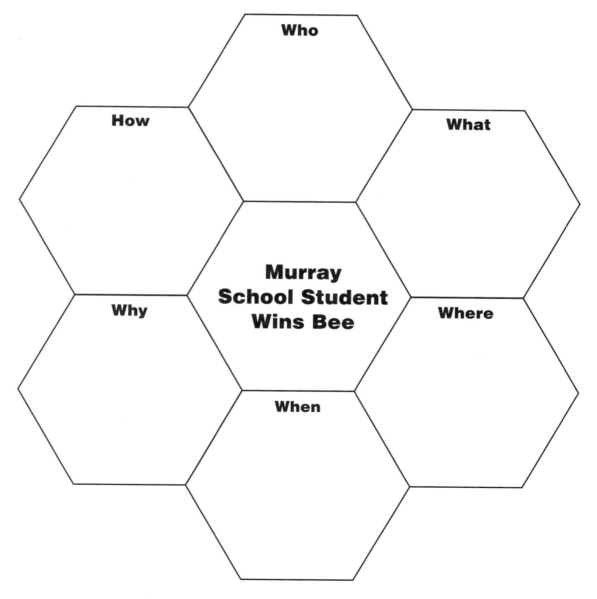

Writing a Good Lead

A. Read each pair of sentences. Check the box next to the sentence that makes a better lead.

1. ☐ Jim Blume's cat likes to climb trees.
   ☐ Jim Blume became a hero last Monday.

2. ☐ Charlie Wong's pickles took first prize at the fair.
   ☐ Charlie Wong won a blue ribbon.

3. ☐ A winter storm on Monday dumped a foot of snow on Cedar Grove.
   ☐ At times, winter storms can bring lots of snow.

B. Read each paragraph. Rewrite the underlined sentence to make a new lead that grabs the reader's attention and tells what happened.

1.   Bay City needed a new theater. The old theater closed last year. For a few months, it sat empty. Then the new owners made big changes. The theater is now ready for business. At the grand opening, movie lovers were smiling.

   _____

   _____

2.   Jane Yolen is a famous author. She gave a talk on Tuesday at two o'clock p.m. The principal greeted her. The Highland School cafeteria was crowded with students and teachers. Everyone came to hear her speak. Some lucky students asked her questions.

   _____

   _____

Adding Details

Read the reporter's notes about something that happened at a zoo. Then read each sentence below. Follow the directions to rewrite the sentence, using details from the notes.

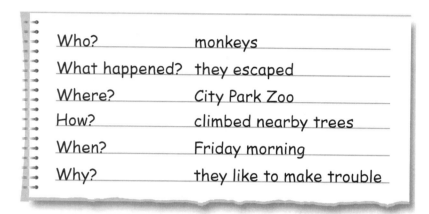

Who?   monkeys

What happened?   they escaped

Where?   City Park Zoo

How?   climbed nearby trees

When?   Friday morning

Why?   they like to make trouble

1. A few animals escaped. (Tell **who** and **where**.)

   _____

   _____

2. Some monkeys were able to get away. (Tell **how**.)

   _____

   _____

3. The clever monkeys got out. (Tell **why**.)

   _____

   _____

4. Something terrible happened at the zoo. (Tell **what** and **when**.)

   _____

   _____

Name: _____

Reviewing a News Article

Revise this news article. Use what you have learned to make it stronger.
Write the news article on a separate sheet of paper.

Focus on:

✓ writing a lead sentence that tells what happened and when

✓ adding details that answer more of the 5Ws and H

Draft

Snow White Is Alive!

The Prince woke Snow White from a deep sleep. It happened yesterday. Snow White stepped out of her glass box. The seven dwarfs cheered. They had thought their friend was dead, because she had eaten a poisoned apple last year. The Prince's kiss woke her. The Prince and Snow White plan to get married next spring.

Writing a Response to Literature

Lesson 1 — Introducing a Response to Literature

A response to literature is writing that responds to a prompt about a reading selection.

1. Explain to students that a quiz or test may call for writing about a story, a passage, or a poem. Say: **Writing about something that you have read is called a *response to literature*. A quiz or test may ask specific questions, or it may just ask you to write your thoughts or ideas about the story. Those questions are called *prompts*.**

2. Read aloud the prompt at the bottom of p. 82. Say: **Think about this question while you read the story.** Then read "Oscar and the Three Otters" as students follow along. If possible, display pictures of otters and seaweed to aid comprehension.

3. Say: **Let's read how one writer responded to the prompt.** Have volunteers take turns reading aloud the response to literature on p. 83. Ask: **What is the purpose of this response to literature?** (to give details that show how Oscar Octopus is rude) Have students write the purpose on the lines provided.

4. Invite students to offer opinions about what makes this a good response to literature. Prompt students by asking: **Does the topic sentence include the title of the story? Does the writer answer the question? Does the writer give three reasons?**

5. Explain that students will use "Oscar and the Three Otters" and the writing model as they study the skills needed to write a good response to literature.

➤ **Extend the Lesson:** Reread the ending to the response on p. 83: *Oscar Octopus is very rude.* Clarify that an ending sentence restates the main idea of the paragraph.

Lesson 2 — Understanding the Prompt

1. Review the purpose of a response to literature.

2. Revisit the prompt on p. 82. Say: **The first step in responding to a story is to figure out what the prompt is asking you to do.** Write the prompt on the board and underline the words *three reasons*. Ask: **What is the prompt asking you to do?** (give three reasons why you do or do not think that Oscar is rude.)

Writing a Response to Literature, continued

Page 85 / Student Book Page 60

Name: _____

Response to Literature

Writing a Topic Sentence

A. Read each prompt. Check the best topic sentence to answer that prompt.

1. **Prompt:** What lesson does the otter family learn in the story?
   - ☑ The family in "Oscar and the Three Otters" learns to lock their door.
   - ☐ The otter family learns a lot about Oscar.

2. **Prompt:** If you were Baby Otter, what would you do at the end of the story?
   - ☑ If I were Baby Otter in "Oscar and the Three Otters," I would let Oscar sleep.
   - ☐ If I were Mama Otter in "Oscar and the Three Otters," I would get angry.

B. Read each story summary and prompt. Write a topic sentence to answer the prompt.

1. "Jack and the Beanstalk" is about a boy who plants magic seeds. They sprout fast. When a beanstalk grows to the sky, Jack climbs it.
   Prompt: Is Jack brave? Tell why you think this.

   In "Jack and the Beanstalk," Jack is brave because he climbs the beanstalk.

2. "The Three Wishes" is about a fisherman who makes three silly wishes without thinking first. His wishes come true.
   Prompt: What is the fisherman's mistake?

   In "The Three Wishes," the fisherman makes a mistake by wasting his wishes.

3. "Little Red Riding Hood" is about a girl who tries to take a basket of food to her grandmother. Along the way, she meets a wolf. Later, the wolf pretends to be the grandmother.
   Prompt: Is the wolf good or bad? Tell why you think so.

   The wolf in "Little Red Riding Hood" is bad because he tries to trick the girl.

© Evan-Moor Corp. • EMC 6012 • Nonfiction Writing   **EXPOSITORY WRITING   85**

Page 86 / Student Book Page 61

Name: _____

Response to Literature

Marking Up the Story

Read the prompt and the story. Do the following to mark up the story:
- ➤ Circle the name of each character in the title.
- ➤ Draw a star next to a word in the title that tells that Fox is smart.
- ➤ Underline the sentence that tells what finally happens to Wolf.

★
The Hungry Wolf and the Clever Fox

Wolf sat under a big yellow moon one night. His stomach growled with hunger. Just then, he saw Fox hurrying to her den. So Wolf blocked the path. He spoke to Fox in a sweet voice. "Fox, you sure look nice tonight."

Fox tried to run past Wolf. "Don't move!" snapped Wolf. "I'm hungry, and you look like a tasty meal."

Fox said, "Why, Mr. Wolf, I'm just skin and bones! But I can show you where to get a big chunk of cheese. Follow me."

Wolf was too hungry to say no. He walked with Fox until they came to a well. Wolf looked down and saw a large, round, yellow cheese floating in the water. He leaned into the well to gobble up the cheese. But he lost his balance and fell into the well.

Fox chuckled. With the help of the full moon, she had outfoxed the wolf.

Prompt: Which character is smarter, Wolf or Fox? Explain how you know.

86   EXPOSITORY WRITING   Nonfiction Writing • EMC 6012 • © Evan-Moor Corp.

---

3. Read aloud the directions for the activity on p. 84. Guide students through the example, modeling how to decide what the prompt is asking for. Clarify that students do not need to answer the prompt itself. If necessary, suggest that students begin each answer with "The prompt asks me to …" or "I have to …" Then have students complete the activity in pairs or small groups. Invite volunteers to share their responses.

➤ **Extend the Lesson:** Provide additional prompts for students to explain, either for the reading selection on p. 82 or for stories that students have read recently.

Lesson 3 Writing a Topic Sentence

1. Say: **When you write a response to literature, begin with a topic sentence that names the story and clearly answers the prompt.**

2. Read aloud the topic sentence in the writing model on p. 83. Ask: **Does this sentence give the title of the story?** (yes) **Does it clearly answer the prompt?** (yes) You may want to discuss other possible topic sentences for the prompt.

3. Read aloud the directions for Activity A on p. 85. Have students complete the activity in small groups.

4. Read the directions for Activity B. Point out that each item is based on a familiar fairy tale or folk tale, and review the stories ("Jack and the Beanstalk," "The Three Wishes," and "Little Red Riding Hood") as needed. Use item 1 to model writing a good topic sentence. Then have students complete the activity in pairs or small groups.

➤ **Extend the Lesson:** Have students write a topic sentence for each prompt on p. 84.

Lesson 4 Marking Up the Story

1. Say: **Once you decide how to answer a prompt, you can look for story details that support your answer. Marking up the story will help you find the details. To mark up a story, you can underline words or sentences, circle them, or highlight them.**

2. Review the prompt on p. 82. Say: **As I read, I'll look for details that show whether Oscar is rude.** Read this sentence: *Oscar Octopus knew that the otters were away. So he crept right into their home.* Say: **This detail shows that Oscar is rude. I'll underline this detail so I can easily find it later.** Continue marking up the story and have students do the same.

3. Direct students to p. 86 and read the instructions for the activity. Then read aloud the story as students follow along. Have students complete the activity.

➤ **Extend the Lesson:** Tell students to draw a box around the word in the story that tells what Wolf mistook for a round wheel of cheese. (moon)

Lesson 5 Using Details from the Story

1. Have students recall how they marked up the story in Lesson 4. Say: **You can use the details that you marked to support your response to literature.**

2. Read a few details from "Oscar and the Three Otters." For each detail, have students give a thumbs up if the sentence shows that Oscar is rude and thumbs down if it does not.

3. Direct students to p. 87. Read aloud the directions for the activity. Then have two or three students take turns reading "The Flute." Use item 1 to model finding details. Say: **I can look back at the story to see how the woodpecker helps Len. The woodpecker says, "I will give you the branch."** Have students complete the activity in pairs. Invite them to share their sentences with the class.

➤ **Extend the Lesson:** Discuss a story that students have read recently. Ask students to tell what they thought of the story and to give details to support their responses.

Lesson 6 Reviewing a Response to Literature

1. Review the qualities of a good response to literature: a topic sentence that names the story and answers the prompt, and details that support the answer.

2. Read aloud the prompt on p. 88. Then read "City Mouse and Country Mouse" as students follow along. Have two students take turns reading the response on p. 89. Then guide students in revising the response. Ask: **Does the topic sentence name the story?** (no) **Does it say how the mice are different?** (no) **Does the writer use three good examples from the story?** (no) **What information does the writer give that does not explain how the mice are different?** (A cat chases the mice, so Country Mouse wants to go back to the country. This is a good story.) Suggest that students omit these sentences from their revisions.

3. Have students write their revisions on a separate sheet of paper. Invite volunteers to share their writing.

Page 87 / Student Book Page 62

Name: _____   Response to Literature

Using Details from the Story

Read the story. Then answer each question, using details from the story.

The Flute

Len was unhappy. Both of his brothers were good at sports. Len wanted to be good at something, too.

One day, Len took a walk in the woods. He heard music and followed the sound to a tall tree. A woodpecker was sitting on a branch. "Where is the music coming from?" Len asked.

"I pecked holes in this branch," the woodpecker said. "The wind makes music when it goes through the holes."

"I wish I could make music like that," Len said.

"I will give you the branch," said the woodpecker.

Len took the flute from the woodpecker. He blew through the holes, but he did not make music.

"Let me teach you how to play," said the woodpecker.

When Len got home, he played his new flute. Everyone loved the music. Len felt happy.

1. How does the woodpecker help Len?
The woodpecker gives the branch to Len and tells him how to play music with it.

2. What makes Len happy at the end of the story?
Len is happy because he can play the flute. Now he is good at something, just like his brothers are.

© Evan-Moor Corp. • EMC 6012 • Nonfiction Writing   **EXPOSITORY WRITING** 87

Pp. 88–89 and Sample Revision / Student Book pp. 63–64

Name: _____   Response to Literature

Name: _____   Response to Literature

Reviewing a Response to Literature

Revise this response to literature. Use what you have learned to make it stronger. Write your response on a separate sheet of paper.
Focus on:
✓ understanding the prompt
✓ writing a topic sentence that answers the prompt and names the story
✓ finding story details that help you answer the prompt
✓ using the story details in your answer

Draft

The mice are different. First, he sleeps on straw in a barn. Second, he gathers

Sample Answer

The two mice in "City Mouse and Country Mouse" are different in three ways. First, Country Mouse sleeps on straw. City Mouse sleeps on cotton cloth. Second, Country Mouse eats plain seeds. City Mouse eats the food that people drop on the floor. Third, Country Mouse likes to feel safe. City Mouse has fun when the cat chases him. The two mice are cousins, but they are not very much alike.

Introducing a Response to Literature

Read this fairy tale.

Oscar and the Three Otters

There once was a family of three otters—Papa Otter, Mama Otter, and Baby Otter. One day, the family left home to go diving deep into the sea for tasty crabs. But the otters forgot to lock their door.

Oscar Octopus knew that the otters were away. So he crept right into their home. Oscar saw three crabs on the table. He took a bite of the biggest crab and spit it out. It was too chewy. Oscar tried the middle-sized crab, but it was too salty. The littlest crab tasted just right, so Oscar ate it all up. Then he saw three beds made from seaweed. The seaweed in one bed was too long. His arms got twisted up in it. The seaweed in another bed was too thick. It felt lumpy. The last bed was just right. Oscar crawled in and fell asleep.

Soon, the three otters came home. They saw bits of crab on the floor. Baby's crab was gone, and Papa's seaweed was in knots. Baby Otter yelled and pointed to the octopus asleep in the seaweed. Oscar woke up. He darted away in a cloud of ink. He did not even say that he was sorry.

Prompt: Is Oscar Octopus rude? Give three reasons why you think this. Use details from the story.

Introducing a Response to Literature

Read this example of a response to literature.

Writing Model

In "Oscar and the Three Otters," Oscar Octopus is rude to the otters. First, he goes into their home when he knows they are away. Second, he eats their crab and messes up their seaweed. Third, he leaves without telling the otters that he is sorry. Oscar Octopus is very rude.

Writer's Purpose: _____

_____

I always leave a thank-you note after I get a snack.

Understanding the Prompt

Read each prompt. Tell what it is asking you to do.

Example

Prompt: Is "Oscar and the Three Otters" a good title for the story? Explain why or why not.

I have to explain why the story title is good or not.

1. **Prompt:** Do you like the story "Oscar and the Three Otters"? Tell why or why not.

   _____

   _____

2. **Prompt:** Compare "Oscar and the Three Otters" to "Goldilocks and the Three Bears." Tell two ways the stories are alike.

   _____

   _____

3. **Prompt:** Why was Oscar Octopus scared at the end of the story?

   _____

   _____

4. **Prompt:** What suggestion would you give the otter family the next time they go diving? Tell how your idea would help.

   _____

   _____

Writing a Topic Sentence

A. Read each prompt. Check the best topic sentence to answer that prompt.

   1. **Prompt:** What lesson does the otter family learn in the story?

     ☐ The family in "Oscar and the Three Otters" learns to lock their door.

     ☐ The otter family learns a lot about Oscar.

   2. **Prompt:** If you were Baby Otter, what would you do at the end of the story?

     ☐ If I were Baby Otter in "Oscar and the Three Otters," I would let Oscar sleep.

     ☐ If I were Mama Otter in "Oscar and the Three Otters," I would get angry.

B. Read each story summary and prompt. Write a topic sentence to answer the prompt.

   1. "Jack and the Beanstalk" is about a boy who plants magic seeds. They sprout fast. When a beanstalk grows to the sky, Jack climbs it.

     Prompt: Is Jack brave? Tell why you think this.

     _____

     _____

   2. "The Three Wishes" is about a fisherman who makes three silly wishes without thinking first. His wishes come true.

     Prompt: What is the fisherman's mistake?

     _____

     _____

   3. "Little Red Riding Hood" is about a girl who tries to take a basket of food to her grandmother. Along the way, she meets a wolf. Later, the wolf pretends to be the grandmother.

     Prompt: Is the wolf good or bad? Tell why you think so.

     _____

     _____

Name: _____

Marking Up the Story

Read the prompt and the story. Do the following to mark up the story:

➤ Circle the name of each character in the title.
➤ Draw a star next to a word in the title that tells that Fox is smart.
➤ Underline the sentence that tells what finally happens to Wolf.

The Hungry Wolf and the Clever Fox

Wolf sat under a big yellow moon one night. His stomach growled with hunger. Just then, he saw Fox hurrying to her den. So Wolf blocked the path. He spoke to Fox in a sweet voice. "Fox, you sure look nice tonight."

Fox tried to run past Wolf. "Don't move!" snapped Wolf. "I'm hungry, and you look like a tasty meal."

Fox said, "Why, Mr. Wolf, I'm just skin and bones! But I can show you where to get a big chunk of cheese. Follow me."

Wolf was too hungry to say no. He walked with Fox until they came to a well. Wolf looked down and saw a large, round, yellow cheese floating in the water. He leaned into the well to gobble up the cheese. But he lost his balance and fell into the well.

Fox chuckled. With the help of the full moon, she had outfoxed the wolf.

Prompt: Which character is smarter, Wolf or Fox? Explain how you know.

Using Details from the Story

Read the story. Then answer each question, using details from the story.

The Flute

Len was unhappy. Both of his brothers were good at sports. Len wanted to be good at something, too.

One day, Len took a walk in the woods. He heard music and followed the sound to a tall tree. A woodpecker was sitting on a branch. "Where is the music coming from?" Len asked.

"I pecked holes in this branch," the woodpecker said. "The wind makes music when it goes through the holes."

"I wish I could make music like that," Len said.

"I will give you the branch," said the woodpecker.

Len took the flute from the woodpecker. He blew through the holes, but he did not make music.

"Let me teach you how to play," said the woodpecker.

When Len got home, he played his new flute. Everyone loved the music. Len felt happy.

1. How does the woodpecker help Len?

_____

_____

2. What makes Len happy at the end of the story?

_____

_____

Name: _____

Reviewing a Response to Literature

Read this fable about two mice.

Reading Selection

City Mouse and Country Mouse

One sunny spring day, City Mouse went to visit his cousin in the country. Country Mouse made a bed of straw in the barn. "You can sleep here, next to me," he told City Mouse. Then Country Mouse gathered seeds. "I've saved the best seeds for you," he told his cousin.

City Mouse stared at the straw. His whiskers twitched when he saw the seeds. "How can you eat such plain food? And how can you sleep in such a rough bed? Come to the city with me. I'll show you how to live."

So the two cousins headed for the city. The sun was setting when they reached the house where City Mouse lived. They pushed through a hole between the bricks to get inside. City Mouse fluffed up a soft cotton cloth. "This is where we will sleep," he said. "But first we'll feast!"

City Mouse led his cousin into the dining room. Bits of cheese, cake, and bread were all over the floor. The mice nibbled until they heard a hiss. "It's the cat!" shouted City Mouse. "Follow me!"

The mice ran through a small hole in the wall. City Mouse laughed and asked, "Wasn't that fun?"

"Not to me!" Country Mouse's heart pounded. "When that cat goes to sleep, I'm leaving. It's better to eat seeds and feel safe than to eat cake and be scared."

Prompt: How are the two mice different? Tell three ways. Use details from the story.

Reviewing a Response to Literature

Revise this response to literature. Use what you have learned to make it stronger. Write your response on a separate sheet of paper.

Focus on:

✓ understanding the prompt

✓ writing a topic sentence that answers the prompt and names the story

✓ finding story details that help you answer the prompt

✓ using the story details in your answer

Draft

The mice are different. First, he sleeps on straw in a barn. Second, he gathers seeds to eat. A cat chases the mice, so Country Mouse wants to go back to the country. This is a good story.

Writing a Research Report

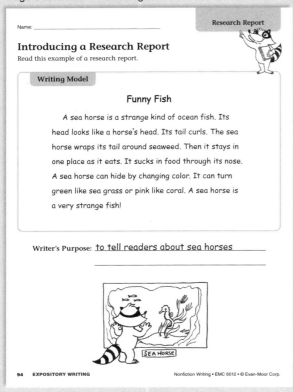

Name: _____

Research Report

Introducing a Research Report
Read this example of a research report.

Writing Model

Funny Fish

A sea horse is a strange kind of ocean fish. Its head looks like a horse's head. Its tail curls. The sea horse wraps its tail around seaweed. Then it stays in one place as it eats. It sucks in food through its nose. A sea horse can hide by changing color. It can turn green like sea grass or pink like coral. A sea horse is a very strange fish!

Writer's Purpose: to tell readers about sea horses _____

94   EXPOSITORY WRITING   Nonfiction Writing • EMC 6012 • © Evan-Moor Corp.

Name: _____

Research Report

Thinking of Questions

Think about each topic and what you might want to find out. Then write three questions to answer in a report.

Example
Topic: sea horses
Questions to answer:
What do sea horses look like?
How do they eat?
How do they stay safe?

1. **Topic:** pandas
Questions to answer:
Where do pandas live?
What do pandas eat?
What makes pandas special?

2. **Topic:** the Statue of Liberty
Questions to answer:
Where is the Statue of Liberty?
How tall is it?
Why is it important?

3. **Topic:** the Grand Canyon
Questions to answer:
Where is the Grand Canyon?
What animals live there?
How many people go to see the Grand Canyon?

© Evan-Moor Corp. • EMC 6012 • Nonfiction Writing   EXPOSITORY WRITING   95

Lesson 1   Introducing a Research Report

A research report is a report that gives details and facts about a topic, using information gathered from different sources.

1. Tell students that the purpose of a research report is to give interesting facts about a topic. Say: **When you want to find out about a topic, you can research by looking in books, magazines, or encyclopedias; looking on the Internet; or asking an expert. You can report on what you find by writing a research report.**

2. Display "Funny Fish" on p. 94. Read aloud the paragraph as students follow along. Have students identify details they think the writer found through research. (e.g., Sea horses wrap their tails around seaweed. They hide by changing color.)

3. Ask: **What is the purpose of this research report?** (to tell readers about sea horses) Have students write the purpose on the lines provided.

4. Invite students to offer opinions about what makes this a good research report. Prompt students by asking: **Is there one sentence that tells you what the report is about? Do all sentences relate to that topic? Do they answer an important question about that topic?**

5. Explain that students will use the model as they study the skills needed to write a good research report.

➤ **Extend the Lesson:** Have students list topics that interest them and that are suitable for a research report.

Lesson 2   Thinking of Questions

1. Review the purpose of a research report. Then say: **Before you begin researching, you need to decide what to find out about your topic. You can start by writing questions you could answer in your report.**

2. Direct students to p. 95. Point out the example and say: **To get started with the report, the writer first wrote a few important questions about sea horses. Then he answered those questions in his report.** Read each question in the example and have students note which sentences in the writing model answer it.

3. Help students complete item 1 by brainstorming questions about pandas. Ask: **What do you think are the most important questions to answer?** Guide students to choose questions that are significant to the topic.

4. Have students work in pairs or small groups to complete items 2 and 3. If necessary, build background about the topics before students begin.

➤ **Extend the Lesson:** Have students write three questions for the topic they chose in the Lesson 1 extension activity.

Lesson 3 Choosing Good Sources

1. Say: **After you write your questions, you're ready to begin researching. You can get information from different *sources*, which can be books, articles, or people.** Provide examples and explain that some sources may be better than others for certain topics. Ask: **Which would be better for learning about clouds—a sports magazine or a book about weather?** (a book about weather)

2. Review "Funny Fish" and the questions in the example on p. 95. Ask: **Where could you go to find answers to these questions?** (e.g., an expert on sea horses, a book about sea horses, a Web site on marine life)

3. Have students complete Activity A on p. 96 in pairs. Review the answers. Discuss why one source is more likely than the other to give information on the topic.

4. Direct students to Activity B and point out that one of the answers is already filled in as an example. Then have students complete the activity in small groups.

➤ **Extend the Lesson:** Have each student find one suitable book, magazine, or Web site to use in researching the topic chosen during the Lesson 1 extension activity.

Lesson 4 Finding Information

1. Review the definition of *source* and say: **Each source gives information in a different way.** Direct students to the sample Web page on p. 97. Say: **Web pages do not all look alike, but most of them have some parts that are similar.** Point out the address bar and explain that this part tells the Web page address. Then note the other parts (title, links, etc.). Point out the encyclopedia entry and say: **An encyclopedia is a set of books (or one book) that contains information about many topics. The topics are in ABC order.**

2. Read aloud the directions for Activity A on p. 97. Then read the Web page text as students follow along. Complete the three questions as a class.

3. Direct students to Activity B and read the entry. Then have students answer the questions in pairs.

Page 96 / Student Book Page 68

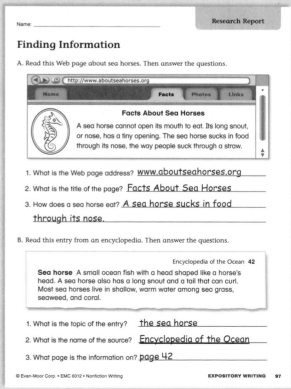

Page 98 / Student Book Page 70

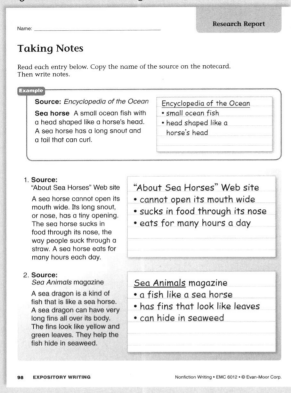

Page 99 / Student Book Page 71

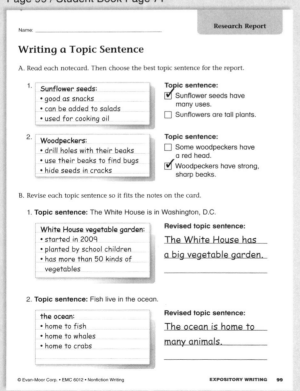

© Evan-Moor Corp. • EMC 6012 • Nonfiction Writing   EXPOSITORY WRITING   99

Lesson 5 Taking Notes

1. Remind students that a *source* is the material in which they will find answers to their research questions.

2. Explain what it means to take notes. Say: **When you take notes, you write down good information that you want to use in your report. You also need to write the name of the source where you find the information.**

3. Direct students to p. 98 and read aloud the encyclopedia entry in the example. Point out that the notecard lists the source and two facts.

4. Ask: **What is the name of the source?** *(Encyclopedia of the Ocean)* Say: **It's important to list the source so you can reread or find more facts later.** Point out that these kinds of notes do not have to be complete sentences.

5. Write these questions on the board: *What do sea horses look like? How do they eat? How do sea horses stay safe?* Refer to the example on p. 98 and ask: **Which of these questions is the writer trying to answer?** (What do sea horses look like?)

6. Complete item 1 as a class, noting the question that the writer is trying to answer. (How do sea horses eat?) Then have students complete item 2 in pairs.

Lesson 6 Writing a Topic Sentence

1. Remind students of the notes they took in Lesson 5. Say: **After a writer takes notes, he or she uses those notes to write sentences for a research report. The first sentence should be a topic sentence. It will tell readers the *main idea* of the report—or what the report is mostly about.**

2. Invite a volunteer to read aloud the topic sentence on p. 94. *(A sea horse is a strange kind of ocean fish.)* Ask: **Does this sentence tell what the report is mostly about?** (yes)

3. Direct students to p. 99. Read aloud the instructions for Activity A and model using item 1. Say: **These notes are all about sunflower seeds. Based on these notes, you can eat sunflower seeds as a snack or put them in salads. The seeds are also used for cooking oil.** Then read the answer choices and ask: **If you were writing a report from these notes, which one of these would be your topic sentence?** Have students complete the activity independently.

4. Read aloud the directions for Activity B. Then read the first notecard. Clarify that the White House is the home of the president of the United States. If possible, display a photo of the White House. Say: **Imagine that you are going to write a report from these notes. Think about the main idea.** Then read the topic sentence and ask: **Why isn't this a good topic sentence?** (It is not about the vegetable garden.) Guide students to revise it. Then complete item 2 as a class.

Lesson 7 Organizing Details

1. Say: **A research report begins with a topic sentence that tells the main idea of the report. The other sentences in the report give details about the topic.**

2. Review the writing model on p. 94 and say: **The details in this report tell what sea horses look like, how they eat, and how they stay safe.**

3. Read aloud the directions on p. 100. Invite a volunteer to read aloud the first topic sentence. Point out that the first notecard lists details about camels. Say: **All of these details are about how camels are able to live in sandy deserts.** Guide students in writing a complete sentence that uses the details on the notecard. Explain that there is more than one way to write the details. When students have finished, invite volunteers to share their sentences.

➤ **Extend the Lesson:** Have students work in small groups to organize the details from the notes on p. 99 and write a paragraph for each topic sentence.

Lesson 8 Reviewing a Research Report

1. Review the qualities of a good research report: a topic sentence, and facts that answer questions about the topic and give information found in different sources.

2. Ask two or three students to read aloud the entry about hedgehogs on p. 101, the notecard, and the draft. Ask: **What is the source?** (the book *Animal Facts*) Draw attention to the notecard and ask: **What question do the notes answer?** (What is a hedgehog?) **Does the draft include all of the facts from the notecard?** (no) **Which ones are missing?** (A hedgehog is a small wild animal; lives in many places in the world.) Read aloud the last sentence and ask: **Does this sentence give a fact?** (no) Discuss how the draft can be improved.

3. Have students write their revisions on a separate sheet of paper. Invite volunteers to share their revised research reports.

Page 100 / Student Book Page 72

Name: _____

Research Report

Organizing Details

Read each topic sentence. Use the details from the notecard to write sentences.

1. Camels can live in sandy deserts.

Their wide, flat feet help them walk in sand. Their thick eyelashes keep the sand out of their eyes. Camels can go for two weeks without drinking water.

Camels:
• wide, flat feet for walking in sand
• thick eyelashes that keep sand out of eyes
• able to go 2 weeks without water

2. It took a lot of work to get the Statue of Liberty to the United States.

The statue was made in France. It was completed in 1884. It was taken apart to be sent on a boat. There were 350 pieces. Workers in New York put the statue together again.

Statue of Liberty:
• made in France
• completed in 1884
• sent in 350 pieces
• put back together in New York

100 EXPOSITORY WRITING

Nonfiction Writing • EMC 6012 • © Evan-Moor Corp.

Page 101 and Sample Revision / Student Book Page 73

Name: _____

Research Report

Reviewing a Research Report

Read the information about hedgehogs. Use it to revise the draft.
Think about what you have learned to make the paragraph stronger.
Write your revision on a separate sheet of paper.

Sample Answer

A hedgehog is a small wild animal with spines. The spines are sharp. A hedgehog keeps itself safe by rolling up into a ball. Hedgehogs live in many parts of the world.

© Evan-Moor Corp. • EMC 6012 • Nonfiction Writing

EXPOSITORY WRITING 93

Name: _____

Introducing a Research Report

Read this example of a research report.

Writing Model

Funny Fish

A sea horse is a strange kind of ocean fish. Its head looks like a horse's head. Its tail curls. The sea horse wraps its tail around seaweed. Then it stays in one place as it eats. It sucks in food through its nose. A sea horse can hide by changing color. It can turn green like sea grass or pink like coral. A sea horse is a very strange fish!

Writer's Purpose: _____

_____

SEA HORSE

   Nonfiction Writing • EMC 6012 • © Evan-Moor Corp.

Name: _____

Thinking of Questions

Think about each topic and what you might want to find out.
Then write three questions to answer in a report.

Topic: sea horses

Questions to answer:

What do sea horses look like?

How do they eat?

How do they stay safe?

1. **Topic:** pandas

   Questions to answer:

   _____

   _____

   _____

2. **Topic:** the Statue of Liberty

   Questions to answer:

   _____

   _____

   _____

3. **Topic:** the Grand Canyon

   Questions to answer:

   _____

   _____

   _____

Choosing Good Sources

A. Answer each question.

1. Who would be better to talk to about elephants—a zookeeper or a beekeeper?

   _____

2. Which would you read to find out about magnets—a cookbook or a science magazine?

   _____

3. Which would you read to find out about the water cycle—a catalog or a book called *All About Rain*?

   _____

4. Where would you go to find out about puppies—a Web site that sells pet food or a pet hospital?

   _____

B. Read each topic. Which source is best for finding information on that topic? Write the number on the line. The first one has been done for you.

Topic		Source
1. grasshoppers	____	a book about ships
2. Benjamin Franklin	____	a Web site on musical instruments
3. drums	____	a beekeeper
4. submarines	____	a book about famous people
5. Washington, D.C.	_1_	an encyclopedia of bugs
6. honey	____	a magazine article on American cities

Finding Information

A. Read this Web page about sea horses. Then answer the questions.

1. What is the Web page address? _____

2. What is the title of the page? _____

3. How does a sea horse eat? _____

_____

B. Read this entry from an encyclopedia. Then answer the questions.

Encyclopedia of the Ocean **42**

Sea horse A small ocean fish with a head shaped like a horse's head. A sea horse also has a long snout and a tail that can curl. Most sea horses live in shallow, warm water among sea grass, seaweed, and coral.

1. What is the topic of the entry? _____

2. What is the name of the source? _____

3. What page is the information on? _____

Name: _____

Taking Notes

Read each entry below. Copy the name of the source on the notecard.
Then write notes.

Source: *Encyclopedia of the Ocean*

Sea horse A small ocean fish with a head shaped like a horse's head. A sea horse has a long snout and a tail that can curl.

Encyclopedia of the Ocean
• small ocean fish
• head shaped like a
  horse's head

1. **Source:**
   "About Sea Horses" Web site

   A sea horse cannot open its mouth wide. Its long snout, or nose, has a tiny opening. The sea horse sucks in food through its nose, the way people suck through a straw. A sea horse eats for many hours each day.

2. **Source:**
   Sea Animals magazine

   A sea dragon is a kind of fish that is like a sea horse. A sea dragon can have very long fins all over its body. The fins look like yellow and green leaves. They help the fish hide in seaweed.

Writing a Topic Sentence

A. Read each notecard. Then choose the best topic sentence for the report.

1.
Sunflower seeds:
• good as snacks
• can be added to salads
• used for cooking oil

Topic sentence:

☐ Sunflower seeds have many uses.

☐ Sunflowers are tall plants.

2.
Woodpeckers:
• drill holes with their beaks
• use their beaks to find bugs
• hide seeds in cracks

Topic sentence:

☐ Some woodpeckers have a red head.

☐ Woodpeckers have strong, sharp beaks.

B. Revise each topic sentence so it fits the notes on the card.

1. **Topic sentence:** The White House is in Washington, D.C.

White House vegetable garden:
• started in 2009
• planted by school children
• has more than 50 kinds of vegetables

Revised topic sentence:

_____

_____

_____

2. **Topic sentence:** Fish live in the ocean.

the ocean:
• home to fish
• home to whales
• home to crabs

Revised topic sentence:

_____

_____

_____

Organizing Details

Read each topic sentence. Use the details from the notecard to write sentences.

1. Camels can live in sandy deserts.

_____

_____

_____

_____

_____

_____

_____

Camels:
- wide, flat feet for walking in sand
- thick eyelashes that keep sand out of eyes
- able to go 2 weeks without water

2. It took a lot of work to get the Statue of Liberty to the United States.

_____

_____

_____

_____

_____

Statue of Liberty:
- made in France
- completed in 1884
- sent in 350 pieces
- put back together in New York

Reviewing a Research Report

Read the information about hedgehogs. Use it to revise the draft.
Think about what you have learned to make the paragraph stronger.
Write your revision on a separate sheet of paper.

Focus on:

✓ starting with a sentence that tells the main idea
✓ giving facts that answer a question
✓ using details from the notes

> Animal Facts **73**
>
> **Hedgehog** A small wild animal that lives in Europe, Asia, Africa, and New Zealand. A hedgehog has sharp spines over most of its body. The spines keep other animals away. When a hedgehog is scared, it rolls itself up into a ball. Then only the spines show, and the hedgehog is protected.

> **Source:** _Animal Facts_
> **What is a hedgehog?**
> • a small wild animal with sharp spines
> • lives in many places
> • rolls itself into a ball to stay safe

Draft

A hedgehog rolls into a ball. It has spines.

The spines are sharp. That is how a hedgehog

stays safe. I think hedgehogs are cute.

Writing a Persuasive Paragraph

Page 105 / Student Book Page 75

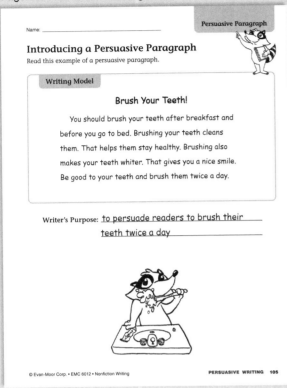

Page 106 / Student Book Page 76

A persuasive paragraph is written to persuade others to agree with the writer or to take a specific action.

1. Invite two or three students to relate an experience in which they tried to persuade their parents to let them do something. Then say: **Another way to persuade people to agree with you or to take a certain action is to put your opinion in writing.**

2. Direct students to p. 105. Say: **This is a persuasive paragraph about brushing your teeth. As you read, focus on the reasons that you should brush your teeth, according to the writer.** Then read aloud "Brush Your Teeth!" as students follow along.

3. Ask: **What is the purpose of this persuasive paragraph?** (to persuade readers to brush their teeth twice a day) Have students write the purpose on the lines provided.

4. Invite students to offer opinions about what makes this a good persuasive paragraph. Prompt students by asking: **Does the writer give an opinion about something? Does he give reasons and examples that make the opinion more convincing? Does the ending state the writer's opinion again?**

5. Explain that students will use the model as they study the skills needed to write a good persuasive paragraph.

➤ **Extend the Lesson:** Have students make a list of topics for a persuasive paragraph.

Lesson 2 **Trying to Persuade**

1. Remind students that the purpose of a persuasive paragraph is to convince the reader to do something. Have students read the first sentence from "Brush Your Teeth!" *(You should brush your teeth …)* and say: **When you are trying to persuade someone to do something, you can use words like *should* and *must*.**

2. Have students read the last sentence of the model paragraph. *(Be good to your teeth and brush them twice a day.)* Explain that this sentence tells someone exactly what to do. Help students identify the two things that the writer is telling them to do. (Be good to your teeth. Brush your teeth.) Say: **When you are trying to persuade others, you can use action words that tell people to do something.**

3. Direct students to p. 106. Read aloud the directions for Activity A and the first pair of sentences. Ask: **Which sentence tells somebody what to do?** (the second one) **What does it say to do?** (Eat fruit every day.) Then have students complete the activity independently.

4. Read aloud the directions for Activity B. Then read the example. Ask: **Which sentence begins with an action word?** *(Put your toys away …)* Then have students complete the activity in pairs.

➤ **Extend the Lesson:** Have students practice writing sentences of their own that begin with action words.

Lesson 3 Writing a Topic Sentence

1. Remind students that a paragraph should always have a *topic sentence,* or a sentence that tells what the paragraph is mostly about. Say: **The topic sentence of a persuasive paragraph also gives an opinion.** Reread the first sentence in "Brush Your Teeth!" and ask: **What is this sentence mostly about?** (brushing teeth) **Does the writer think you *should* or should *not* brush your teeth?** (He thinks you should.)

2. Read the directions for Activity A on p. 107. Read the first paragraph and ask: **What is this paragraph about?** (doing chores) **What is the writer's opinion?** (that kids should do chores at home) Read the answer choices and ask: **Which possibility uses persuasive language?** (the second one) **Does that choice tell what the paragraph is about?** (yes) Have students complete the activity independently or in pairs.

3. Read the directions for Activity B and model using the first item. Have students complete the activity in pairs.

➤ **Extend the Lesson:** Ask students questions such as *Should we go to the museum or the park for a class trip?* Have students write an answer that expresses an opinion.

Lesson 4 Giving Reasons

1. Say: **A persuasive paragraph tells the writer's opinion about a topic and includes reasons for that opinion.**

2. Revisit the topic sentence on p. 105 and say: **The writer believes we should brush our teeth twice a day.** Read the next sentence: *Brushing your teeth cleans them.* Ask: **Is this a good reason to brush our teeth twice a day?** (yes) Challenge students to identify another reason. (makes your teeth whiter) Point out that some details (e.g., the third sentence) provide support for the reasons.

Page 107 / Student Book Page 77

Name: _____

Persuasive Paragraph

Writing a Topic Sentence

A. Each paragraph has a missing topic sentence. Read the paragraph. Then check the box next to the best topic sentence to begin the paragraph.

1. _____ It is easy to dust or sweep the floor. It does not take long to throw out the trash, either. Everyone can help at home.
   ☐ Kids hate to do chores at home.
   ☑ Kids should do simple chores at home.

2. _____ Teachers and students use computers for many things. But sometimes the computer lab is locked. If every classroom had its own computers, we could use them every day.
   ☐ Computers are useful.
   ☑ All classrooms should have computers.

3. _____ Movies about people in danger can be scary. Monsters in movies can be scary, too. Scary movies give you bad dreams.
   ☑ Do not watch scary movies before you go to bed.
   ☐ Movies about sharks are scary.

B. Read each paragraph. Rewrite the underlined sentence so it gives an opinion and tells the main idea of the paragraph.

1. Chocolate is a type of candy. Candy tastes good, but it is not a healthful food. Candy usually has lots of sugar. For most people, it is OK to eat some candy as a treat but not often.

   Do not eat too much candy.

2. Dogs with short hair may be cold in winter. Some people put clothes on their pets. They think the clothes look cute. Most pets do not like to wear clothes, though. Clothes are for people, not for pets.

   Do not make your pets wear clothes.

© Evan-Moor Corp. • EMC 6012 • Nonfiction Writing   PERSUASIVE WRITING   107

Page 108 / Student Book Page 78

Name: _____

Persuasive Paragraph

Giving Reasons

A. Read each opinion. Check the box next to the best reason for that opinion.

1. **Opinion:** Our second-grade class should have a pet.
   ☐ Parrots are beautiful and smart.
   ☑ We would learn more about animals.

2. **Opinion:** Kids need about ten hours of sleep each night.
   ☑ Our bodies and brains need rest.
   ☐ Some kids go to bed at eight o'clock at night.

3. **Opinion:** Eat snacks that are good for you.
   ☐ Grapes are best when they are frozen.
   ☑ Your body needs healthful food so it can grow strong.

B. Read each opinion. Write two reasons for that opinion.

1. **Opinion:** Everyone should have a pet.
   Reason: Pets keep people from being lonely.
   Reason: Pets make people happy.

2. **Opinion:** Kids should exercise every day.
   Reason: Exercise makes you stronger.
   Reason: Exercise keeps you in good shape.

108   PERSUASIVE WRITING   Nonfiction Writing • EMC 6012 • © Evan-Moor Corp.

Page 109 / Student Book Page 79

Page 110 and Sample Revision / Student Book Page 80

3. Read the directions for Activity A on p. 108. Then read the first item and ask: **Which sentence gives a better reason why the class should have a pet?** *(We would learn more about animals.)* Have students complete the activity independently. Check the answers together.

4. Read the directions for Activity B. Then read the first item. Brainstorm reasons why people get pets. Then ask students to choose two reasons and write them in the boxes. Have students complete item 2 in small groups. Then invite them to share their responses.

➤ **Extend the Lesson:** Have students complete a graphic organizer for one of the topics they brainstormed in the Lesson 1 extension activity. Have them write an opinion and then give one or two reasons for it.

Lesson 5 Writing a Conclusion

1. Say: **The final sentence in a persuasive paragraph is your last chance to persuade readers.** Read the last sentence of the writing model. Then review the topic sentence and explain: **The conclusion states the topic again and gives the writer's opinion in a new way.**

2. Direct students to p. 109. Use the first item to model the activity. Say: **The topic sentence is** *You should play outside every day.* **To write a good conclusion, I need to say nearly the same thing but in a different way, and I also need to be persuasive. I'll write** *Play outdoors often and enjoy yourself.* Then have students complete the activity in pairs.

➤ **Extend the Lesson:** Have students write a new conclusion for the model paragraph on p. 105.

Lesson 6 Reviewing a Persuasive Paragraph

1. Review the qualities of a good persuasive paragraph: a topic sentence that states an opinion, reasons that support the opinion, and a concluding sentence that restates the opinion in a persuasive way.

2. Read aloud "Be Smart! Wear a Bike Helmet!" on p. 110 as students follow along. Then guide students through revising the draft. Ask: **Does the first sentence tell readers to do something?** (no) **Has the writer given the most important reason for wearing a bike helmet?** (no) **Does the last sentence state the opinion again?** (no)

3. Have students write their revisions on a separate sheet of paper. Invite volunteers to share their revisions.

Name: _____

Introducing a Persuasive Paragraph

Read this example of a persuasive paragraph.

Writing Model

Brush Your Teeth!

You should brush your teeth after breakfast and before you go to bed. Brushing your teeth cleans them. That helps them stay healthy. Brushing also makes your teeth whiter. That gives you a nice smile. Be good to your teeth and brush them twice a day.

Writer's Purpose: _____

_____

Trying to Persuade

A. Read each pair of sentences. Check the box next to the sentence that tells you to do something.

1. ☐ Fruit is good for you.
   ☐ Eat fruit every day for good health.

2. ☐ You should wash your hands before each meal.
   ☐ Clean hands can stop germs from spreading.

3. ☐ Dogs like to go for walks.
   ☐ You must walk your dog every morning.

4. ☐ Stop at every red light.
   ☐ Red lights tell drivers to stop.

5. ☐ You must take turns when you play this game.
   ☐ This is a good game for two or more players.

B. Rewrite each sentence so it tells someone what to do. Start your sentence with an action word.

> **Example**
>
> It is hard to find toys in a messy room.
>
> <u>Put your toys away when you finish playing</u>.

1. Breakfast is important.

   _____

2. Litter goes in the trash can.

   _____

3. A good way to make friends is to play a team sport.

   _____

Name: _____

Writing a Topic Sentence

A. Each paragraph has a missing topic sentence. Read the paragraph. Then check the box next to the best topic sentence to begin the paragraph.

1. _____ It is easy to dust or sweep the floor. It does not take long to throw out the trash, either. Everyone can help at home.

☐ Kids hate to do chores at home.

☐ Kids should do simple chores at home.

2. _____ Teachers and students use computers for many things. But sometimes the computer lab is locked. If every classroom had its own computers, we could use them every day.

☐ Computers are useful.

☐ All classrooms should have computers.

3. _____ Movies about people in danger can be scary. Monsters in movies can be scary, too. Scary movies give you bad dreams.

☐ Do not watch scary movies before you go to bed.

☐ Movies about sharks are scary.

B. Read each paragraph. Rewrite the underlined sentence so it gives an opinion and tells the main idea of the paragraph.

1. <u>Chocolate is a type of candy.</u> Candy tastes good, but it is not a healthful food. Candy usually has lots of sugar. For most people, it is OK to eat some candy as a treat but not often.

_____

2. <u>Dogs with short hair may be cold in winter.</u> Some people put clothes on their pets. They think the clothes look cute. Most pets do not like to wear clothes, though. Clothes are for people, not for pets.

_____

Giving Reasons

A. Read each opinion. Check the box next to the best reason for that opinion.

1. **Opinion:** Our second-grade class should have a pet.

   ☐ Parrots are beautiful and smart.
   ☐ We would learn more about animals.

2. **Opinion:** Kids need about ten hours of sleep each night.

   ☐ Our bodies and brains need rest.
   ☐ Some kids go to bed at eight o'clock at night.

3. **Opinion:** Eat snacks that are good for you.

   ☐ Grapes are best when they are frozen.
   ☐ Your body needs healthful food so it can grow strong.

B. Read each opinion. Write two reasons for that opinion.

1. **Opinion:** Everyone should have a pet.

   Reason: _____

   Reason: _____

2. **Opinion:** Kids should exercise every day.

   Reason: _____

   Reason: _____

Writing a Conclusion

Read each paragraph. Then write a concluding sentence that retells the topic sentence in a different way.

1.   <u>You should play outside every day.</u> Run, kick a ball, ride a bike, dance, or climb. These activities make your muscles strong. And they make you feel good.

_____

2.   <u>We should take a class trip to the fire station.</u> We can see the firetrucks. The firefighters can show us how they get ready to fight fires. They can teach us about safety.

_____

3.   <u>All kids should be able to have a pet.</u> Pets help kids learn to be kind. Pets help kids learn to take care of animals. Pets are also good friends.

_____

4.   <u>You should eat vegetables every day.</u> Vegetables have important vitamins. Your body needs these to stay healthy. Carrots, spinach, and other veggies make the body's systems work better.

_____

5.   <u>Do your homework in a quiet place.</u> Then you can think only about your work. You will make fewer mistakes. And you will finish your work faster, too.

_____

Reviewing a Persuasive Paragraph

Revise this persuasive paragraph. Use what you have learned to make it stronger. Write your paragraph on a separate sheet of paper.

Focus on:
- ✓ writing a topic sentence that gives an opinion
- ✓ giving reasons for the opinion
- ✓ writing an ending that retells the topic in a persuasive way

Draft

Be Smart! Wear a Bike Helmet!

You can wear a helmet when you ride your bike. That is probably a good thing to do. Even good riders fall down sometimes. Besides, helmets look cool. They come in all types and colors.

Writing a Persuasive Letter

Lesson 1 Introducing a Persuasive Letter

A persuasive letter is a letter written to persuade someone to agree with the writer or to take a specific action.

1. Say: **If you want to convince someone to do something, you can write a persuasive letter.**

2. Direct students to p. 114 and explain that this letter is from a student to a school principal. Ask: **Who wrote it?** (Marty O'Toole) Say: **As you read the letter, focus on why Marty wants to bring pets to school for the day.** Read aloud the letter as students follow along.

3. Ask: **To whom did Marty write this letter?** (Principal Alright) Explain that the principal is the writer's audience. If necessary, define *audience*. Ask: **What is the purpose of this letter?** (to persuade the principal to allow a Pet Day at school) Have students write the audience and purpose on the lines provided.

4. Invite students to offer opinions about what makes this a good persuasive letter. Prompt students by asking: **Does the first sentence state what Marty wants? Does Marty try to persuade Principal Alright to do something? Does he explain why? Does he include all of the necessary parts of a letter, such as a greeting?**

5. Explain that students will use the model as they study the skills needed to write good persuasive letters.

➤ **Extend the Lesson:** Have students make a list of actions they might persuade others to take. (e.g., have a track-and-field day or games day at school)

Lesson 2 Knowing Your Audience

1. Remind students that the purpose of a persuasive letter is to persuade someone to do something. Say: **When you write a persuasive letter, you need to think about who will read it. You need to make sure that what you are asking for is something that the person can really do.** Ask: **Would you ask your parents to build a new playground at the park?** (no) Say: **Your parents wouldn't be able to do that, so this would not be a good topic for a letter to them.** Ask: **What could you ask your parents for?** (e.g., new clothes, a toy or game, a special meal)

2. Review the writing model on p. 114 and remind students that the letter is to Principal Alright. Ask: **What does Marty want Principal Alright to do?** (allow a Pet Day at school) **Is that something a principal can do?** (yes)

Page 114 / Student Book Page 82

Name: _____

Persuasive Letter

Introducing a Persuasive Letter
Read this example of a persuasive letter.

> **Writing Model**
>
> May 20, 2012
>
> Dear Principal Alright,
>
> We would like to have a special day at school when we could bring our pets. Animals make people happy. Students will do better in class if they are happy. We will keep our pets on leashes or in cages. And we will clean up after them. Please consider letting us have a Pet Day at school.
>
> Sincerely,
>
> Marty O'Toole

Writer's Audience: _Principal Alright_

Writer's Purpose: _to persuade the principal to allow a Pet Day at school_

114 PERSUASIVE WRITING   Nonfiction Writing • EMC 6012 • © Evan-Moor Corp.

Page 115 / Student Book Page 83

Name: _____   Persuasive Letter

Knowing Your Audience

A. Read each topic for a persuasive letter. Then write the number of each
   topic next to the audience that goes with that topic.

Topic

1. getting a new pet
2. having a longer recess
3. building a playground at the city park
4. changing your softball team's name

Audience

__4__ your softball coach
__1__ your parents
__2__ your principal
__3__ the mayor

B. Read each question. Notice the words in bold type. Think of a good topic
   for a persuasive letter you could write to that person.

Example

What can you ask **your parents** to help you with?
I can ask them to help me with my homework.

1. What can you ask **your teacher** to let you do?
   I can ask my teacher to let me feed the class pet.

2. What can you ask **a firefighter** to do for you?
   I can ask a firefighter to show me the firetruck.

3. What can you ask **your friends** to do?
   I can ask my friends to see the play I am in.

4. What can you ask **the president of the United States** to do?
   I can ask the president to do a good job.

© Evan-Moor Corp. • EMC 6012 • Nonfiction Writing   PERSUASIVE WRITING   115

Page 116 / Student Book Page 84

Name: _____   Persuasive Letter

Giving Reasons

A. Read each letter. Then check the box next to the reason that is
   more persuasive.

1. Dear President of Fantastic Figures,
   I think you should make action figures that cannot break. I own
   many of your action figures. But my sister breaks them when she
   plays with them.
   ☑ My parents would buy more action figures for me if the toys did not
     break so easily.
   ☐ I think you should make toys for little sisters, too.

2. Dear Aunt Jenny,
   I am learning to play the guitar. Mom said you have an old guitar
   you do not play anymore. I would like to use it for my guitar lessons.
   ☐ I will give it back to you after a few months.
   ☑ I will practice hard and play a song just for you.

3. Dear Principal Sanchez,
   I think you should fix the broken computers in the lab. Some of the
   keyboards do not work. Some of the computers are too slow.
   ☐ If you fix the computers, we can play more games.
   ☑ If you fix the computers, we can use them to do our homework.

B. Read this persuasive letter. Then add another good reason that Mom
   and Dad should buy a new bike for you.

Dear Mom and Dad,
   I need a new bike. My old bike has wobbly wheels and a rusty
   chain. It is hard to pedal and hard to steer.
I will be safer on a new bike.

_____

116   PERSUASIVE WRITING   Nonfiction Writing • EMC 6012 • © Evan-Moor Corp.

---

3. Read aloud the directions for Activity A on p. 115 and
   have students complete the activity independently.
   Invite volunteers to share their responses and explain
   their thinking.

4. Discuss the example for Activity B. Brainstorm topics
   with students or have them complete the activity in
   small groups. Review student responses together.

➤ **Extend the Lesson:** Have students work in pairs to
   name other people they might write persuasive letters to
   and give an appropriate topic for each person.

Lesson 3 Giving Reasons

1. Say: **The first sentence in your letter should say
   what you want the person to do for you. Remember,
   you want that person to agree with you.**

2. Read the first sentence of the model letter on p. 114
   and ask: **What does Marty want?** (a special day when
   students can bring pets to school) Explain that even
   though this sentence alone may not persuade the
   principal, it clearly states what Marty wants.

3. Say: **When you write a persuasive letter, include
   good reasons for what you want. Ask: Why does
   Marty think a Pet Day is a good idea? What are his
   reasons?** (Animals make people happy. Kids would do
   better in class.) **Are these good reasons?** (yes)

4. Read this sentence from p. 114: *We will keep our pets on
   leashes or in cages.* **Do you think most principals
   would be worried about pets making a mess or
   getting loose?** (yes) **Why do you think Marty wrote
   this sentence in his letter?** (so Principal Alright won't
   worry about the pets making a mess or getting loose)
   Say: **When you write a persuasive letter, include
   reasons that the *audience* will think are good.**

5. Direct students to Activity A on p. 116. Read aloud the
   instructions and the letter to the president of Fantastic
   Figures. If necessary, explain what an action figure is.
   Then say: **This letter is not finished yet. The writer
   needs to include a good reason why the company
   should make action figures that don't break.** Guide
   students to choose the more effective reason. Then
   have them complete the activity independently.

6. Read aloud the directions for Activity B. Have students
   complete the activity in pairs or small groups.

➤ **Extend the Lesson:** Have students write persuasive
   sentences for two or three items on p. 115, choosing
   reasons that are appropriate for the audience and topic.

Lesson 4 Organizing Your Letter

1. Say: **A persuasive letter, like most letters, includes certain parts.** Point out the following parts of a letter, using the writing model: date, greeting, body, closing, and signature. Ask: **In what other ways can you close a letter besides saying *Sincerely*?** (e.g., *Love, Yours truly, Regards*) Discuss which closings are most appropriate for each audience. (e.g., *Love* for parents or grandparents, *Sincerely* for the principal)

2. Review punctuation in a letter. Point out that the greeting ends with a comma. Ask: **Which other line in a letter always ends with a comma?** (the closing)

3. Discuss the sentences that make up the body of the letter on p. 114. Point out that the first sentence tells what Marty wants, the next few sentences include persuasive reasons, and the ending sentence repeats what the first sentence asks for.

4. Read the directions for Activity A on p. 117 and have students complete the activity independently or in pairs. Check the answers together.

5. Have students complete Activity B independently.

➤ **Extend the Lesson:** Explain that persuasive letters to people you know well can be formatted like friendly letters. You may want to show how to format business letters, however, for more formal persuasive letters.

Lesson 5 Reviewing a Persuasive Letter

1. Review the qualities of a good persuasive letter: the correct parts of the letter (date, greeting, body, closing, and signature); a sentence that states what you want; reasons that will appeal to the audience; and an ending that restates what you want.

2. Read aloud the letter on p. 118 as students follow along. Then guide students through revising the draft. Ask: **Who is the audience?** (author Ms. Schachner) **Does the first sentence say what the writer wants?** (yes) **Does the writer give good reasons?** (no) **How can you change it so the reasons are better?** (e.g., say that kids will buy more books if the author visits) **Are any parts of the letter missing?** (Yes. The date is missing, and the ending sentence is missing from the body of the letter.) **Is the closing the best one to use when writing to someone you don't know very well?** (no) **Are any commas missing?** (yes)

3. Have students write their revised letters on a separate sheet of paper. Invite volunteers to share their letters.

Page 117 / Student Book Page 85

Name: _____   Persuasive Letter

Organizing Your Letter

A. Label each part of the letter. Use the words in the box.

| date | greeting | body | closing | signature |

closing ____ Sincerely,

greeting ____ Dear Mr. Watkins,

date ____ October 5, 2012

signature ____ *Ellie Funt*

body ____ Our second-grade class should take a trip to the zoo. A zoo has animals from around the world. We can find out how the animals eat, sleep, and play. The zoo is a good place for us to learn about animals.

B. Write the letter from Activity A. Put the parts in the correct order.

October 5, 2012

Dear Mr. Watkins,

Our second-grade class should take a trip to the zoo. A zoo has animals from around the world. We can find out how the animals eat, sleep, and play. The zoo is a good place for us to learn about animals.

Sincerely,
Ellie Funt

© Evan-Moor Corp. • EMC 6012 • Nonfiction Writing   PERSUASIVE WRITING 117

Page 118 and Sample Revision / Student Book Page 86

Name: _____   Persuasive Letter

Reviewing a Persuasive Letter

Revise this persuasive letter. Use what you have learned to make it stronger. Write your persuasive letter on a separate sheet of paper.

Sample Answer

September 21, 2012

Dear Ms. Schachner,

Please come talk to our class. You are our favorite author. We love your books about Skippyjon Jones! You could tell us about writing stories. We would like to know how you invent names that are fun to say, like Mr. Doodlepaws and Pickle Pants. We would be very happy if you came. We would like to ask you some questions, too. We know you are busy, but we hope you can visit.

Sincerely,

Mrs. Ortega's Second Graders
Sally Ride School

Name: _____

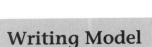

Introducing a Persuasive Letter

Read this example of a persuasive letter.

Writing Model

May 20, 2012

Dear Principal Alright,

   We would like to have a special day at school when we could bring our pets. Animals make people happy. Students will do better in class if they are happy. We will keep our pets on leashes or in cages. And we will clean up after them. Please consider letting us have a Pet Day at school.

Sincerely,

Marty O'Toole

Writer's Audience: _____

Writer's Purpose: _____

_____

Knowing Your Audience

A. Read each topic for a persuasive letter. Then write the number of each topic next to the audience that goes with that topic.

Topic

1. getting a new pet

2. having a longer recess

3. building a playground at the city park

4. changing your softball team's name

Audience

_____ your softball coach

_____ your parents

_____ your principal

_____ the mayor

B. Read each question. Notice the words in bold type. Think of a good topic for a persuasive letter you could write to that person.

> **Example**
>
> What can you ask **your parents** to help you with?
>
> I can ask them to help me with my homework.

1. What can you ask **your teacher** to let you do?

_____

2. What can you ask **a firefighter** to do for you?

_____

3. What can you ask **your friends** to do?

_____

4. What can you ask **the president of the United States** to do?

_____

Giving Reasons

A. Read each letter. Then check the box next to the reason that is more persuasive.

1. Dear President of Fantastic Figures,

    I think you should make action figures that cannot break. I own many of your action figures. But my sister breaks them when she plays with them.

    ☐ My parents would buy more action figures for me if the toys did not break so easily.

    ☐ I think you should make toys for little sisters, too.

2. Dear Aunt Jenny,

    I am learning to play the guitar. Mom said you have an old guitar you do not play anymore. I would like to use it for my guitar lessons.

    ☐ I will give it back to you after a few months.

    ☐ I will practice hard and play a song just for you.

3. Dear Principal Sanchez,

    I think you should fix the broken computers in the lab. Some of the keyboards do not work. Some of the computers are too slow.

    ☐ If you fix the computers, we can play more games.

    ☐ If you fix the computers, we can use them to do our homework.

B. Read this persuasive letter. Then add another good reason that Mom and Dad should buy a new bike for you.

Dear Mom and Dad,

    I need a new bike. My old bike has wobbly wheels and a rusty chain. It is hard to pedal and hard to steer.

_____

_____

Name: _____

Organizing Your Letter

A. Label each part of the letter. Use the words in the box.

date	_____	Sincerely,
greeting	_____	Dear Mr. Watkins,
body	_____	October 5, 2012
closing	_____	*Ellie Funt*
signature	_____	Our second-grade class should take a trip to the zoo. A zoo has animals from around the world. We can find out how the animals eat, sleep, and play. The zoo is a good place for us to learn about animals.

B. Write the letter from Activity A. Put the parts in the correct order.

_____

_____

_____

_____

_____

_____

_____

Reviewing a Persuasive Letter

Revise this persuasive letter. Use what you have learned to make it stronger. Write your persuasive letter on a separate sheet of paper.

Focus on:

✓ writing for your audience
✓ using all parts of a letter
✓ using the first and last sentences to say what you want
✓ using commas where you need to

Draft

Dear Ms. Schachner

   Please come talk to our class. You are our favorite author. We love your books about Skippyjon Jones! How do you write your stories? We want to know how you invent names that are fun to say, like Mr. Doodlepaws and Pickle Pants. We would like to ask you questions, too.

                    Bye,

                    Mrs. Ortega's Second Graders
                    Sally Ride School

Writing a Review

Lesson 1 Introducing a Review

A review gives important information and the writer's opinion about a book, movie, show, restaurant, or product.

1. Ask students to think of books they have read, games they have played, or movies they have seen recently. Invite volunteers to complete these sentence frames:

   I like _____ because _____.

   I do not like _____ because _____.

   Explain that a good way to share information and opinions about something is to write a review.

2. Read aloud "An Adventure Game" on p. 122 as students follow along. Ask: **What is this review about?** (a video game called *Peter Pan's Adventures*)

3. Ask: **What is the purpose of this review?** (to share information and opinions about a video game called *Peter Pan's Adventures*) Then have students write the purpose on the lines provided.

4. Invite students to offer opinions about what makes this a good review. Prompt students by asking: **Does the first sentence tell what is being reviewed? Does the review give facts and opinions? Does the writer recommend the game?**

5. Explain that students will use the model as they study the skills needed to write a good review.

➤ **Extend the Lesson:** Have students read book reviews posted by online children's book clubs.

Lesson 2 Writing a Beginning

1. Review the purpose of a review.

2. Say: **Writers usually begin their reviews by telling what they are reviewing and giving an opinion about it. An opinion tells what someone thinks or feels.**

3. Read aloud the first sentence of the review on p. 122. Have students underline the name of the product (*Peter Pan's Adventures*) and the words that tell what it is (*video game*). Ask: **Why is it important for the reviewer to tell what is being reviewed?** (e.g., so you know what the writer is talking about) **What opinion does the writer give about the video game?** (It's fun.)

4. Ask: **Can you write a review of something that you do not like?** (yes) Clarify that a review can be positive or negative.

Page 122 / Student Book Page 88

Name: _____

Review

Introducing a Review
Read this example of a review.

Writing Model

An Adventure Game

The video game *Peter Pan's Adventures* is fun. You get to help Peter Pan save his friends, the Lost Boys. The game is not easy. First you have to help Peter find his shadow. Then you search for clues to find the boys. The game is never boring. It is a good game for almost anyone.

Writer's Purpose: to share information and opinions about a video game called *Peter Pan's Adventures*

122 PERSUASIVE WRITING

Nonfiction Writing • EMC 6012 • © Evan-Moor Corp.

Page 123 / Student Book Page 89

Name: _____ Review

Writing a Beginning

A. Read each pair of sentences. Check the sentence that is best for the beginning of a review.

1. ☐ *Space Trail* costs $60.
   ☑ *Space Trail* is a fun video game to play with friends.

2. ☐ I went to Panda Garden for my birthday.
   ☑ Panda Garden is a good restaurant for lunch.

3. ☐ I watched *Patty Pony* three times.
   ☑ *Patty Pony* is a funny movie about a horse named Patty.

4. ☑ The book *Pinocchio* tells the sad story of a boy.
   ☐ I read the book *Pinocchio* yesterday.

B. Name things you can review. Then write the first sentence of each review.

1. A book that I have read: Shiver Me Timbers
   Shiver Me Timbers is a great book if you like ghost stories.

2. A TV show that I have seen: Animal Adventure Camp
   Animal Adventure Camp is an interesting TV show about wild animals.

3. A toy, game, or app that I have played: Doodle Town
   Doodle Town is a fun app to play if you like puzzles.

© Evan-Moor Corp. • EMC 6012 • Nonfiction Writing   PERSUASIVE WRITING   123

Page 124 / Student Book Page 90

Name: _____ Review

Adding Facts and Opinions

A. Read each sentence. Write **F** if it is a fact. Write **O** if it is an opinion.

1. F The TV show about Posey the cat is shown on Saturday mornings.
2. O The TV show about Posey the cat will make you laugh.
3. O This robot is the best toy of all.
4. F This toy robot has parts that move.

B. Write an example of each topic. Then write a fact and an opinion about it.

1. A board game that I have played: checkers
   Fact: Checkers is a board game for two players.
   Opinion: Checkers is an easy game to learn.

2. A sport that I have watched: basketball
   Fact: A basketball is orange.
   Opinion: Basketball is exciting to watch.

3. A place that I have visited: Legoland
   Fact: There are many rides at Legoland.
   Opinion: Legoland is fun for kids of all ages.

4. A book or story that I have read: Why the Sea Is Salt
   Fact: This folk tale is about two brothers.
   Opinion: The story has a sad ending.

124   PERSUASIVE WRITING   Nonfiction Writing • EMC 6012 • © Evan-Moor Corp.

---

5. Read aloud the directions for Activity A on p. 123. Then read aloud the first pair of sentences and ask: **What product is being reviewed?** *(Space Trail)* **What is it?** (a video game) **What does the reviewer think about it?** (It's fun.) Guide students to recognize that the best sentence to begin a review with is the one that gives all of this information. Then have students complete the activity independently.

6. Read the directions for Activity B. Brainstorm specific books; TV shows; and toys, games, and apps that students can write about. Then have students complete the activity in pairs or small groups. Invite volunteers to share their sentences with the class.

➤ **Extend the Lesson:** Have students state a positive opinion and a negative opinion about a toy, game, book, movie, TV show, or restaurant they know about.

Lesson 3 Adding Facts and Opinions

1. Say: **Writers give both facts and opinions to add details to their reviews.** Remind students that an opinion is what someone thinks or feels. Say: **A fact is a statement that can be proved.**

2. Read this sentence from the model on p. 122: *The game is not easy.* Ask: **Is this sentence a fact or an opinion?** (opinion) Encourage students to explain. (You cannot prove that the game is not easy. It may be easy for some and difficult for others.) Then read this sentence from the model: *First you have to help Peter find his shadow.* Ask: **Is this a fact or an opinion?** (fact) Explain that it is a fact because it describes a step in the game.

3. Point out that giving a reason for an opinion makes that opinion more valuable. Say: **The writer describes how to play the game so we will understand why he says that it is not easy.**

4. Read aloud the directions for Activity A on p. 124. Have students complete the activity independently or in pairs. Discuss the answers as a class.

5. Read the directions for Activity B. Give examples of board games for item 1 (e.g., Candy Land, Sorry!, Monopoly). Then brainstorm places that students can review for item 3 (e.g., a local park, playground, or museum). Have students complete the activity independently or in pairs. Then invite volunteers to share their sentences with the class.

➤ **Extend the Lesson:** Have pairs of students write a fact and an opinion about a familiar toy.

Lesson 4 Writing an Ending

1. Say: **A review usually ends with one last opinion about what the writer is reviewing. Sometimes the writer makes a recommendation, such as "Don't bother seeing this movie" or "I recommend this book for kids who are interested in dinosaurs." A good ending can sum up the ideas in the review.**

2. Read aloud the last sentence of "An Adventure Game" on p. 122 and ask: **Does the writer recommend this video game?** (yes) **Who does he think will enjoy it?** (almost anyone)

3. Direct students to p. 125. Model the activity using the first item. Read the review and ask: **Does the writer like Krispy Kangaroo cereal?** (yes) **Why?** (It is tasty, good for you, and crunchy.) **Do you think the writer would recommend this cereal? If so, why?** Explore suitable endings for the review. (e.g., Krispy Kangaroo cereal is a healthful breakfast or snack, anyone who likes crunchy foods will enjoy eating this cereal.) Say: **Remember, a good ending gives an opinion.** Then have students complete the activity in pairs or small groups. Invite volunteers to share their sentences with the class.

Lesson 5 Reviewing a Written Review

1. Review the qualities of a good review: a beginning sentence that tells what is being reviewed and gives an opinion, facts and opinions that add details, and an ending that gives one last opinion about the thing being reviewed.

2. Read aloud "Gobs of Problems" on p. 126 as students follow along. Then guide students through revising the draft. Ask: **What product is being reviewed?** (Gobs of Gumballs) **Does the first sentence give an opinion?** (yes) **Does it tell the name of the product?** (yes) **Does it explain what it is?** (no) Then say: **The first sentence says that the kit has many problems, but the review mentions only two.** Ask: **What other problems might a gumball-making kit have?** (e.g., The flavors may be awful, the colors may be ugly, the gum may be too sticky.) Write the ideas on the board and suggest that students include one or two in their revisions. Then ask: **Does the last sentence give an opinion?** (no) **What recommendation would you make?** (that people not buy the kit)

3. Have students write their revisions on a separate sheet of paper. Invite volunteers to share their reviews.

Name: _____

Review

Writing an Ending

Read each review. Then write a good ending for it.

1. Krispy Kangaroo is a tasty cereal. It is good for you, too. It does not get soggy when you pour milk on it. This cereal is crunchy!

   People should eat Krispy Kangaroo cereal because it tastes good.

2. Magic Bubble Wand is not a good toy. The bubble soap does not make good bubbles. They pop too quickly. The plastic wand is so thin that it breaks easily.

   People should not buy Magic Bubble Wand, because it does not work very well.

3. *Dogs and Cats* is a fun computer game. The animals look and act like real dogs and cats. The game is easy to learn.

   Dogs and Cats is a good game for anyone who likes pets.

4. The TV show *Dinosaur Land* is boring. It is full of people talking about dinosaurs. The show never shows any dinosaurs.

   This TV show would be better if it had more dinosaurs.

5. The butterfly museum is a great place to visit. Hundreds of beautiful butterflies fly freely. The inside garden is warm and quiet. Sometimes butterflies land on you.

   If you like butterflies, you will enjoy the butterfly museum.

© Evan-Moor Corp. • EMC 6012 • Nonfiction Writing   **PERSUASIVE WRITING** 125

Name: _____

Review

Reviewing a Written Review

Revise this review of a gumball-making kit. Use what you have learned to make it stronger. Write your review on a separate sheet of paper.

Focus on:

Sample Answer

Gobs of Problems

"Gobs of Gumballs" is a gumball-making kit that has many problems. The directions are hard to follow. There isn't enough sugar to make the gumballs. The flavors are yucky, too. Who wants to chew a sour celery gumball? I do not think people should buy this kit, because it is a waste of money.

126

Name: _____

Introducing a Review

Read this example of a review.

Writing Model

An Adventure Game

The video game *Peter Pan's Adventures* is fun. You get to help Peter Pan save his friends, the Lost Boys. The game is not easy. First you have to help Peter find his shadow. Then you search for clues to find the boys. The game is never boring. It is a good game for almost anyone.

Writer's Purpose: _____

_____

_____

Writing a Beginning

A. Read each pair of sentences. Check the sentence that is best for the beginning of a review.

1. ☐ *Space Trail* costs $60.
   ☐ *Space Trail* is a fun video game to play with friends.

2. ☐ I went to Panda Garden for my birthday.
   ☐ Panda Garden is a good restaurant for lunch.

3. ☐ I watched *Patty Pony* three times.
   ☐ *Patty Pony* is a funny movie about a horse named Patty.

4. ☐ The book *Pinocchio* tells the sad story of a boy.
   ☐ I read the book *Pinocchio* yesterday.

B. Name things you can review. Then write the first sentence of each review.

1. A book that I have read: _____

   _____

   _____

2. A TV show that I have seen: _____

   _____

   _____

3. A toy, game, or app that I have played: _____

   _____

   _____

Name: _____

Adding Facts and Opinions

A. Read each sentence. Write **F** if it is a fact. Write **O** if it is an opinion.

1. ___ The TV show about Posey the cat is shown on Saturday mornings.

2. ___ The TV show about Posey the cat will make you laugh.

3. ___ This robot is the best toy of all.

4. ___ This toy robot has parts that move.

B. Write an example of each topic. Then write a fact and an opinion about it.

1. A board game that I have played: _____

   Fact: _____

   Opinion: _____

2. A sport that I have watched: _____

   Fact: _____

   Opinion: _____

3. A place that I have visited: _____

   Fact: _____

   Opinion: _____

4. A book or story that I have read: _____

   Fact: _____

   Opinion: _____

Name: _____

Writing an Ending

Read each review. Then write a good ending for it.

1. Krispy Kangaroo is a tasty cereal. It is good for you, too. It does not get soggy when you pour milk on it. This cereal is crunchy!

    _____

    _____

2. Magic Bubble Wand is not a good toy. The bubble soap does not make good bubbles. They pop too quickly. The plastic wand is so thin that it breaks easily.

    _____

    _____

3. *Dogs and Cats* is a fun computer game. The animals look and act like real dogs and cats. The game is easy to learn.

    _____

    _____

4. The TV show *Dinosaur Land* is boring. It is full of people talking about dinosaurs. The show never shows any dinosaurs.

    _____

    _____

5. The butterfly museum is a great place to visit. Hundreds of beautiful butterflies fly freely. The inside garden is warm and quiet. Sometimes butterflies land on you.

    _____

    _____

Name: _____

Reviewing a Written Review

Revise this review of a gumball-making kit. Use what you have learned to make it stronger. Write your review on a separate sheet of paper.

Focus on:
- ✓ telling what the product is and what you think of it
- ✓ giving facts and more opinions about it
- ✓ writing an ending that has one last opinion

Draft

Gobs of Problems

"Gobs of Gumballs" has many problems.

The directions are hard to follow. There

isn't enough sugar to make the gumballs.

You can buy this kit if you want to.

Writing a Personal Narrative

Lesson 1 Introducing a Personal Narrative

A personal narrative is writing that tells about a specific event or experience from the writer's own life.

1. Ask students if they have ever had a memorable experience with a wild animal, such as a deer or a raccoon. Invite a few students to tell their stories. Then say: **You can tell an interesting story from your life in a personal narrative.**

2. Direct students to the personal narrative on p. 130, "Bandit Stinks!" Read it aloud as students follow along.

3. Ask: **What is the purpose of this personal narrative?** (to tell about something that happened to a pet dog named Bandit) Have students write the purpose on the lines provided.

4. Ask: **What is the topic of this personal narrative?** (a skunk spraying a dog named Bandit) Have students identify the topic sentence. *(One night last …)* Point out that it introduces the topic of the personal narrative.

5. Invite students to offer opinions about what makes this a good personal narrative. Prompt students by asking: **Does the story tell about one specific event? Can you picture some of the details in your mind? Did the writer include his own thoughts and feelings about what happened? Are the details in order?**

6. Explain that students will use the model as they study the skills needed to write a personal narrative.

➤ **Extend the Lesson:** Have students brainstorm topics for their own personal narratives.

Lesson 2 Choosing a Specific Topic

1. Review the purpose of a personal narrative. Say: **A good personal narrative is about one specific event. Good writers think about a specific topic before they begin to write.** Present the examples below and discuss them with the class.

Not specific enough: *my summer vacation*
Specific: *building a sand castle with my big sister*
Not specific enough: *shopping*
Specific: *the time I got lost in a department store*

---

2. Review the topic of the model on p. 130 and ask: **Is the topic specific?** (yes)

3. Have students complete Activity A on p. 131 in small groups. Review the answers together.

Page 130 / Student Book Page 94

Name: _____

Personal Narrative

Introducing a Personal Narrative
Read this example of a personal narrative.

Writing Model

Bandit Stinks!

One night last summer, a skunk sprayed Bandit, my pet beagle. Bandit was in the backyard. Late that night, he started howling. He sounded so sad! When Dad opened the door, Bandit ran inside. The smell of rotten cabbage followed. I thought Bandit was going to stink up the whole house! Finally, Dad trapped Bandit in the bathroom. All the noise woke Mom up. That made her grumpy. Bandit caused a lot of trouble that night.

Writer's Purpose: to tell about something that happened to a pet dog named Bandit

130   NARRATIVE WRITING   Nonfiction Writing • EMC 6012 • © Evan-Moor Corp.

Page 131 / Student Book Page 95

Name: _____

Personal Narrative

Choosing a Specific Topic

A. Read each pair of topics. Check the most specific one.

1. ☐ things to do at the beach and park
   ☑ tossing stones into the ocean

2. ☐ telling how bikes are made
   ☑ getting a bike for my seventh birthday

3. ☑ feeding baby goats at the zoo
   ☐ school field trips

B. Read the topics. They are not specific enough. Write a better, more specific topic for each one.

Example
Topic: the first day of school
getting lost in the halls

1. **Topic:** earning money
   saving the money I earned to buy my sister a gift

2. **Topic:** soccer
   the first time I made a goal in a soccer game

3. **Topic:** a visit with a relative
   when I learned to make biscuits at my grandma's house

4. **Topic:** pets
   the day I came home with a puppy

© Evan-Moor Corp. • EMC 6012 • Nonfiction Writing   NARRATIVE WRITING   131

Writing a Personal Narrative, continued

Page 132 / Student Book Page 96

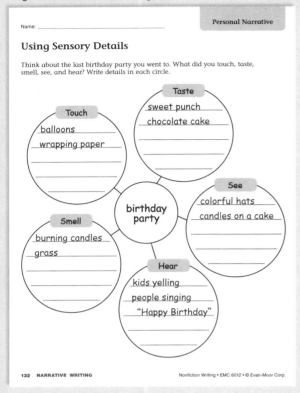

Page 133 / Student Book Page 97

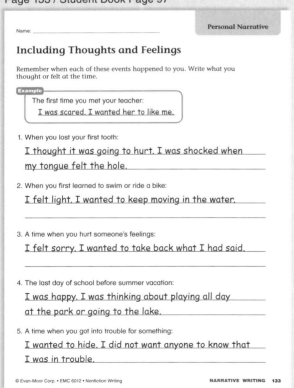

4. Read aloud the directions for Activity B and the example. Ask: **What specific things could you write about that happened to you on your first day of school?** (e.g., sitting next to someone new, meeting the teacher) Have students complete the activity in pairs or independently. Invite volunteers to share their topics.

➤ **Extend the Lesson:** Have partners evaluate the topics they brainstormed in the Lesson 1 extension activity, deciding which are specific enough and which are not.

Lesson 3 Using Sensory Details

1. Say: **A good personal narrative uses details that describe things you can touch, taste, smell, see, or hear. These kinds of details help readers imagine the event or topic.**

2. Have students underline sensory details in "Bandit Stinks!" (*started howling, smell of rotten cabbage, noise woke Mom up*, etc.)

3. Direct students to p. 132 and ask: **What do you see at a birthday party?** (balloons, hats, gifts) **What might you taste?** (cake, ice cream) Then have students complete the activity independently or in pairs.

➤ **Extend the Lesson:** Have students make a sensory details web for their own personal narrative topic.

Lesson 4 Including Thoughts and Feelings

1. Explain that in a personal narrative, the writer describes an event and also tells his or her thoughts and feelings about the event.

2. Review the model on p. 130 and ask: **Which sentences tell what the writer thought or felt that night when Bandit got sprayed by a skunk?** (*He sounded so sad! I thought Bandit was going to stink up the whole house! That made her grumpy. Bandit caused a lot of trouble that night.*)

3. Ask: **How did you feel when you met your first-grade teacher for the first time?** Invite two or three students to briefly describe how they felt. Say: **When you write what you think and feel about an event, it helps readers understand your experience.**

4. Direct students to p. 133. Read aloud the instructions and discuss the example. Then have students complete the activity independently or in pairs.

➤ **Extend the Lesson:** Have students brainstorm thoughts and feelings to include in their personal narratives.

Lesson 5 Organizing Details

1. Say: **Personal narratives usually follow time order. Writers give the details of the event in the order they occurred.** Review signal words that show sequence (e.g., *first, then, next, finally*).

2. Draw a timeline for the writing model on p. 130. Prompt students to identify story details to show on the timeline. (e.g., Bandit starts howling. Dad opens door.) As you label the timeline, note that the story reveals the details in sequential order.

3. Say: **Organizing details is like making a sandwich. The slices of bread are the beginning and ending. The details are the fillings. You can stack the fillings in the order that makes the most sense.**

4. Read aloud the directions for Activity A on p. 134. Clarify that students should write the numbers in the circles on the sandwich. Have students complete the activity independently or in pairs. Review the answers and ask students to explain their thinking.

5. Have students complete Activity B independently. Then have two or three volunteers take turns reading aloud the rewritten paragraph.

➤ **Extend the Lesson:** Have students make a graphic organizer and use it to record beginning and ending sentences and details for their own personal narratives.

Lesson 6 Reviewing a Personal Narrative

1. Review the qualities of a good personal narrative: a specific topic, sensory details, thoughts and feelings about the topic, and a clear order of events.

2. Read "Riding to Ben's House" on p. 135 as students follow along. Then guide students through revising the draft. Ask: **Does the first sentence tell about riding to Ben's house?** (no) Note that the fourth sentence *(Once, I rode my bike …)* introduces the topic but doesn't say when it happened. Then ask: **Does the writer say how he felt when he was chased by the dog?** (no) Prompt students to name things that the bike rider might have heard, touched, smelled, or tasted on the ride to Ben's house.

3. Have students write their revised personal narratives on a separate sheet of paper. Invite volunteers to share their revisions with the class.

Page 134 / Student Book Page 98

Name: _____

Personal Narrative

Organizing Details

A. Read the sentences. Think about the order of the events. Then write the number of each sentence to show when the event happens in the story.

1. Last night, I gave my cat Tigger a bath.

2. Tigger hissed and moaned as we rinsed her clean.

3. First, Mom held Tigger down as I poured water on her.

4. Finally, Tigger was clean, and Mom and I were very tired.

5. Then I rubbed pink shampoo into Tigger's fur.

What, no cheese?

1 — beginning

3

5 middle

2

4 — end

B. Rewrite this paragraph in the order that the events happen.

First, I found an old fishbowl to use as the tadpole's home. Then I walked to the pond behind our house. For my science project, I wanted to raise a tadpole into a frog. I could hardly wait for a frog to grow! Finally, I put the tadpole into its new home. I splashed around until I caught a wiggly tadpole.

For my science project, I wanted to raise a tadpole into a frog. First, I found an old fishbowl to use as the tadpole's home. Then I walked to the pond behind our house. I splashed around until I caught a wiggly tadpole. Finally, I put the tadpole into its new home. I could hardly wait for a frog to grow!

134 NARRATIVE WRITING
Nonfiction Writing • EMC 6012 • © Evan-Moor Corp.

Page 135 and Sample Revision / Student Book Page 99

Name: _____

Personal Narrative

Reviewing a Personal Narrative

Revise this personal narrative. Use what you have learned to make it stronger. Write the personal narrative on a separate sheet of paper.

Focus on:

Sample Answer

Riding to Ben's House

Last week, I rode my bike alone to my friend Ben's house. At first, it was fun. Then a huge dog jumped out from behind a bush. It chased me all the way down the street. Its bark was loud and deep. I was so scared! I rode as fast as I could. Sweat ran down my back. Finally, the dog gave up. When I got to Ben's street, I rode over a big hole in the road. My bike wobbled and I almost fell. I finally got to Ben's house. But it seemed like it took forever.

Introducing a Personal Narrative

Read this example of a personal narrative.

Writing Model

Bandit Stinks!

One night last summer, a skunk sprayed Bandit, my pet beagle. Bandit was in the backyard. Late that night, he started howling. He sounded so sad! When Dad opened the door, Bandit ran inside. The smell of rotten cabbage followed. I thought Bandit was going to stink up the whole house! Finally, Dad trapped Bandit in the bathroom. All the noise woke Mom up. That made her grumpy. Bandit caused a lot of trouble that night.

Writer's Purpose: _____

_____

Choosing a Specific Topic

A. Read each pair of topics. Check the most specific one.

1. ☐ things to do at the beach and park
   ☐ tossing stones into the ocean

2. ☐ telling how bikes are made
   ☐ getting a bike for my seventh birthday

3. ☐ feeding baby goats at the zoo
   ☐ school field trips

B. Read the topics. They are not specific enough. Write a better, more specific topic for each one.

Example

Topic: the first day of school
<u>getting lost in the halls</u>

1. **Topic:** earning money

   _____

2. **Topic:** soccer

   _____

3. **Topic:** a visit with a relative

   _____

4. **Topic:** pets

   _____

Using Sensory Details

Think about the last birthday party you went to. What did you touch, taste, smell, see, and hear? Write details in each circle.

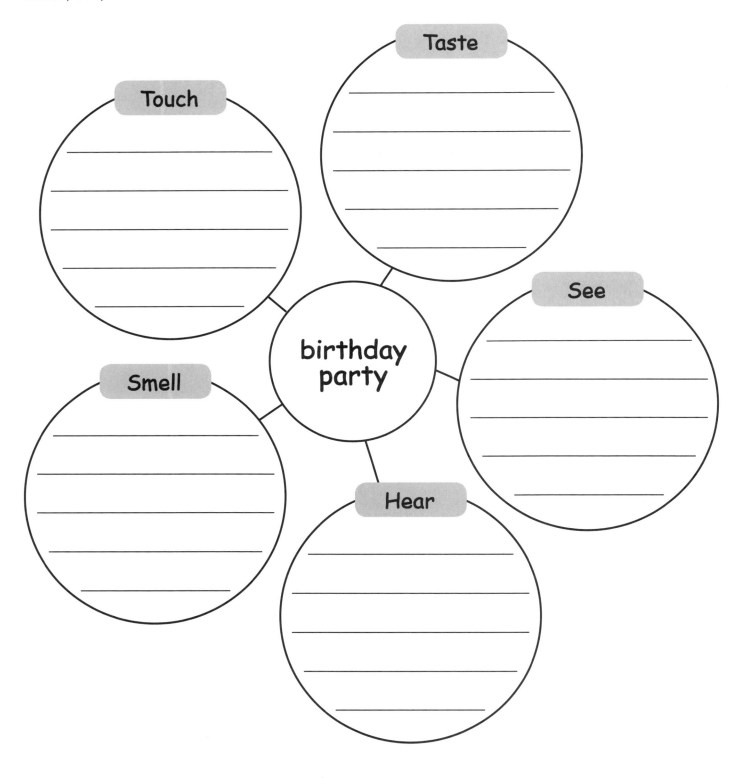

Including Thoughts and Feelings

Remember when each of these events happened to you. Write what you thought or felt at the time.

Example

The first time you met your teacher:

I was scared. I wanted her to like me.

1. When you lost your first tooth:

_____

_____

2. When you first learned to swim or ride a bike:

_____

_____

3. A time when you hurt someone's feelings:

_____

_____

4. The last day of school before summer vacation:

_____

_____

5. A time when you got into trouble for something:

_____

_____

Organizing Details

A. Read the sentences. Think about the order of the events. Then write the number of each sentence to show when the event happens in the story.

1. Last night, I gave my cat Tigger a bath.

2. Tigger hissed and moaned as we rinsed her clean.

3. First, Mom held Tigger down as I poured water on her.

4. Finally, Tigger was clean, and Mom and I were very tired.

5. Then I rubbed pink shampoo into Tigger's fur.

What, no cheese?

— beginning

middle

— end

B. Rewrite this paragraph in the order that the events happen.

First, I found an old fishbowl to use as the tadpole's home. Then I walked to the pond behind our house. For my science project, I wanted to raise a tadpole into a frog. I could hardly wait for a frog to grow! Finally, I put the tadpole into its new home. I splashed around until I caught a wiggly tadpole.

_____

_____

_____

_____

_____

Reviewing a Personal Narrative

Revise this personal narrative. Use what you have learned to make it stronger. Write the personal narrative on a separate sheet of paper.

Focus on:

✓ telling about one specific topic
✓ writing details that tell how something sounds, feels, looks, smells, or tastes
✓ including thoughts and feelings about the topic
✓ putting the details in the order they happened

Draft

Riding to Ben's House

I ride my bike a lot. My mom always tells me to wear my helmet. My dad always tells me to look out for cars. Once, I rode my bike alone to my friend Ben's house. At first, I rode slowly. Then a huge dog jumped out from behind a bush. It chased me all the way down the street. Then I rode faster. I finally got to Ben's house.

Writing a Friendly Letter

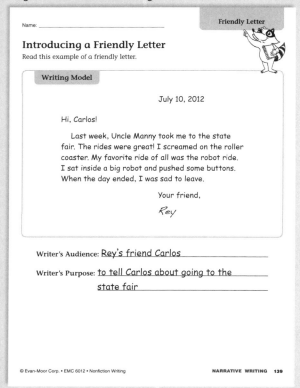

Lesson 1 Introducing a Friendly Letter

A friendly letter is a letter that tells about something personal in the writer's life. It is written to someone the writer knows well.

1. Ask students how they communicate with friends and family members they don't see every day. (e.g., phone calls, text messages, letters) Say: **One way we can keep in touch with friends and family members who live far away is to write friendly letters. You can write about things that you have done.**

2. Direct students to the writing model on p. 139. Read aloud the letter as students follow along.

3. Ask: **Who wrote this letter?** (Rey) **To whom did he write it?** (his friend Carlos) Explain that Carlos is the writer's audience. Define *audience* if necessary. Ask: **What is the purpose of this friendly letter?** (to tell Carlos about going to the state fair) Have students write the audience and purpose on the lines provided.

4. Invite students to offer opinions about what makes this a good friendly letter. Prompt students by asking: **Can you tell why Rey is writing to Carlos? Does the letter stick to the topic? Are the details interesting? Does Rey share his thoughts and feelings about the topic?**

5. Explain that students will use the model as they study the skills needed to write a good friendly letter.

➤ **Extend the Lesson:** Point out that friendly letters can have the same purpose as e-mail. Let students share what they know about using e-mail. Help them compare and contrast these two forms.

Lesson 2 Writing for Your Audience

1. Say: **You can write a friendly letter to someone you know well.** Have students brainstorm people to whom they might send a friendly letter. (e.g., personal friend, relative, family friend) Then ask: **Would you send a friendly letter to the owner of a grocery store?** (no) **Why not?** (That person is a stranger.)

2. Refer to p. 139 and remind students of the audience. Ask: **How do we know Carlos and Rey are friends?** (Rey closes with "Your friend." He begins with "Hi.")

3. Ask: **What is the subject of Rey's letter?** (going to the state fair) **Is this a good topic for a letter to a friend?** (yes) Explain: **This is a good topic because it probably is something that interests Carlos. When you write a friendly letter, choose a topic that the audience is interested in.**

4. Direct students to p. 140 and have them complete Activity A independently.

5. Read aloud the directions for Activity B and use the first item to model. Read the topic and say: **I would write a letter to my sister because she likes parties a lot.** Then have students complete the activity independently or in pairs. Invite volunteers to share their sentences.

6. Have students complete Activity C in pairs or small groups. Invite them to share their lists with the class.

➤ **Extend the Lesson:** Have students copy the chart and use it as they brainstorm good topics for friendly letters to different people they know.

Lesson 3 Adding Details

1. Review the purpose of a friendly letter. Say: **When you write about an event in a friendly letter, it is important to include interesting details. It is also important to stay on topic.**

2. Point out details in the model on p. 139. Ask: **What was Rey's favorite ride at the state fair?** (the robot ride) **What other ride did he go on?** (roller coaster) Give students an opportunity to tell which details they find most interesting. Then ask: **Does Rey write only about the things he did at the fair?** (yes) Say: **Rey stayed on topic and wrote only about this one experience of going to the fair.**

3. Read aloud the directions for Activity A on p. 141 and complete the first item with students. Read the letter aloud and ask: **What is the topic?** (a baseball game last Saturday) Read the answer choices aloud and ask: **Which detail is more interesting for Kevin to read?** (the one about sliding into third base) **Does it stay on topic?** (yes) Have students complete the activity independently. Review the answers and have students explain their choices.

4. Guide students through Activity B. Ask: **What is the topic of Tess's letter?** (her new kitten) **Which sentences are not about that topic?** (*Our neighbors have a dog …* and *My favorite channel …*) Then ask: **What else could Tess tell Abigail about Roxy?** (e.g., what Roxy looks like, what Tess thinks of Roxy) Have students complete the activity independently.

➤ **Extend the Lesson:** Have partners write two or more sentences with interesting details they might include in a friendly letter about a pet.

Page 140 / Student Book Page 102

Name: _____

Friendly Letter

Writing for Your Audience

A. Circle three people to whom you are most likely to send a friendly letter.

(your cousin)   the owner of a supermarket   (a grandparent)
(your friend)   the mayor of your city   your dentist

B. Read each topic. Think of someone you know who would like to get a letter about that topic. Complete the sentence and tell why you would write to that person.

1. **Topic:** your last birthday party
   I would write a letter to _my cousin in Springfield because her birthday is the same week as mine_ .

2. **Topic:** a vacation with your family
   I would write a letter to _my friend Dylan because he likes to swim, and my family went to a good lake for swimming_ .

3. **Topic:** a class field trip
   I would write a letter to _the school principal to tell her how much we liked the field trip to the shoe factory_ .

C. Think about topics for a friendly letter. List two topics for each audience.

my best friend	my grandparents
getting a new bike	getting a good report card
finding a bird's nest	acting in the school play

140   NARRATIVE WRITING   Nonfiction Writing • EMC 6012 • © Evan-Moor Corp.

Page 141 / Student Book Page 103

Name: _____

Friendly Letter

Adding Details

A. Read each friendly letter. Check the box next to the sentence that adds an interesting detail about the topic.

1. Dear Kevin,
   My baseball game last Saturday was great. When it was my turn at bat, I hit the ball all the way to the back fence.
   ☐ There were a hundred cars in the parking lot.
   ☑ I slid into third base, and the umpire yelled "Safe!"

2. Dear Grandma,
   I took my new camera with me when we went to Big Bend. There are interesting plants and animals there. I can send you some photos.
   ☐ The pool at the hotel had a slide.
   ☑ My favorite photo shows a bird sitting on a cactus.

3. Dear Tina,
   Yesterday I planted a tree at school. My sister helped. It was hard work!
   ☑ First, my sister and I dug a hole big enough for the tree roots.
   ☐ Maple trees lose their leaves at the end of autumn.

B. Read this friendly letter. Cross out two sentences that are not about the topic. Write two sentences with details that Tess could include.

Dear Abigail,
   I got a surprise on my birthday. Mom gave me a kitten! I named the kitten Roxy. Her fur is soft and light. ~~Our neighbors have a dog named Rosey.~~ After dinner, Roxy sleeps in my lap while I watch TV. ~~My favorite channel has cartoons.~~ I hope you can meet Roxy!

                                   Love,
                                   Tess

Her fur is black, but she has white paws.

Roxy is the best gift I ever got!

© Evan-Moor Corp. • EMC 6012 • Nonfiction Writing   **NARRATIVE WRITING**   141

Page 142 / Student Book Page 104

Name: _____

Friendly Letter

Sharing Thoughts and Feelings

Read each topic. Write a thought or feeling you have about the topic.

Example

Topic: watching cartoons

I am happy when I can stay in my pajamas and watch cartoons.

1. **Topic:** the first day of school

   I was glad to see my friends again. _____

2. **Topic:** a park where you have played

   I am scared to climb the ropes at the park. _____

3. **Topic:** a video game you have played

   I think Treasure Hunt is hard to play. _____

4. **Topic:** a birthday party you went to

   I felt proud to win the beanbag toss. _____

5. **Topic:** an animal or a pet

   I think a hamster is the best pet. _____

142 NARRATIVE WRITING   Nonfiction Writing • EMC 6012 • © Evan-Moor Corp.

Page 143 and Sample Revision / Student Book Page 105

Name: _____

Friendly Letter

Reviewing a Friendly Letter

Revise this friendly letter. Use what you have learned to make it stronger.
Write the letter on a separate sheet of paper.

Sample Answer

January 11, 2012

Dear Cassie,

   I had a great birthday party! We played pin the tail on the pony. Then we decorated horseshoes. I used purple puffy paint and red glitter on mine. We all had so much fun! Mom made my birthday cake. She put green coconut and small toy ponies on it. It was beautiful. I'm sorry that you missed my party.

Love,

Mia

Lesson 4 Sharing Thoughts and Feelings

1. Say: **When you share your thoughts and feelings in a friendly letter, the person reading the letter knows how you feel about the topic.**

2. Direct students to the model on p. 139 and read the first two sentences. Ask: **Which sentence tells how Rey feels about the state fair?** (the second one) Then have students look for another sentence in which Rey expresses his feelings. *(When the day ended, I was sad to leave.)* Ask: **What feeling does he express?** (sadness)

3. Read aloud the directions for the activity on p. 142 and guide students through the example. Say: **The topic is "watching cartoons." Ask: What do you think about cartoons? How do you feel when you are watching them?** Explain that the writer feels happy, and invite volunteers to suggest other possibilities. Encourage students to make statements that do not begin with "I think" or "I feel." Have them complete the activity independently or in pairs. Invite volunteers to share their sentences with the class.

➤ **Extend the Lesson:** Have students circle each word or phrase that expresses a thought or feeling in the sentences they wrote. (e.g., *happy*, *difficult*, or *best*)

Lesson 5 Reviewing a Friendly Letter

1. Review the qualities of a good friendly letter: a topic that is appropriate for the audience, interesting details that stay on topic, and sentences that tell the writer's thoughts and feelings.

2. Read aloud the friendly letter on p. 143 as students follow along. Then guide students through the revision. Ask: **What is the topic of the letter?** (Mia's birthday party) **Is it a good topic for the audience?** (yes) **Do all of the sentences stay on topic?** (no) **Which ones do not?** (*At school, sometimes my friends …* and *Jenn always runs the fastest.*) Tell students to omit those sentences from their revisions. Then ask: **What other details might interest Cassie?** Point out that Mia mentions the cake but doesn't say what flavor it is or what it looks like. Ask: **Does Mia express any thoughts or feelings about her party?** (no) **Do you think she enjoyed it?** (yes) **Did Cassie come to the party?** (no)

3. Have students write their revised letters on a separate sheet of paper. Invite volunteers to share their revisions with the class.

Name: _____

Introducing a Friendly Letter

Read this example of a friendly letter.

Writing Model

July 10, 2012

Hi, Carlos!

   Last week, Uncle Manny took me to the state fair. The rides were great! I screamed on the roller coaster. My favorite ride of all was the robot ride. I sat inside a big robot and pushed some buttons. When the day ended, I was sad to leave.

   Your friend,

   Rey

Writer's Audience: _____

Writer's Purpose: _____

_____

Writing for Your Audience

A. Circle three people to whom you are most likely to send a friendly letter.

your cousin   the owner of a supermarket   a grandparent

your friend   the mayor of your city   your dentist

B. Read each topic. Think of someone you know who would like to get a letter about that topic. Complete the sentence and tell why you would write to that person.

1. **Topic:** your last birthday party

   I would write a letter to _____

   _____.

2. **Topic:** a vacation with your family

   I would write a letter to _____

   _____.

3. **Topic:** a class field trip

   I would write a letter to _____

   _____.

C. Think about topics for a friendly letter. List two topics for each audience.

my best friend	my grandparents

Adding Details

A. Read each friendly letter. Check the box next to the sentence that adds an interesting detail about the topic.

1. Dear Kevin,

    My baseball game last Saturday was great. When it was my turn at bat, I hit the ball all the way to the back fence.

    ☐ There were a hundred cars in the parking lot.

    ☐ I slid into third base, and the umpire yelled "Safe!"

2. Dear Grandma,

    I took my new camera with me when we went to Big Bend. There are interesting plants and animals there. I can send you some photos.

    ☐ The pool at the hotel had a slide.

    ☐ My favorite photo shows a bird sitting on a cactus.

3. Dear Tina,

    Yesterday I planted a tree at school. My sister helped. It was hard work!

    ☐ First, my sister and I dug a hole big enough for the tree roots.

    ☐ Maple trees lose their leaves at the end of autumn.

B. Read this friendly letter. Cross out two sentences that are not about the topic. Write two sentences with details that Tess could include.

Dear Abigail,

    I got a surprise on my birthday. Mom gave me a kitten! I named the kitten Roxy. Her fur is soft and light. Our neighbors have a dog named Rosey. After dinner, Roxy sleeps in my lap while I watch TV. My favorite channel has cartoons. I hope you can meet Roxy!

                                        Love,
                                        Tess

_____

_____

Sharing Thoughts and Feelings

Read each topic. Write a thought or feeling you have about the topic.

Example

Topic: watching cartoons

<u>I am happy when I can stay in my pajamas and watch cartoons.</u>

1. **Topic:** the first day of school

_____

_____

2. **Topic:** a park where you have played

_____

_____

3. **Topic:** a video game you have played

_____

_____

4. **Topic:** a birthday party you went to

_____

_____

5. **Topic:** an animal or a pet

_____

_____

Reviewing a Friendly Letter

Revise this friendly letter. Use what you have learned to make it stronger.
Write the letter on a separate sheet of paper.

Focus on:
✓ adding interesting details about the topic
✓ sharing thoughts and feelings about the topic

Draft

January 11, 2012

Dear Cassie,

Saturday was my birthday party. We played pin the tail on the pony. Then we decorated horseshoes. I used purple puffy paint and red glitter on mine. At school, sometimes my friends and I run around like ponies. Jenn always runs the fastest. Mom made my birthday cake.

Love,
Mia

Writing a Journal Entry

Name: _____

Journal Entry

Introducing a Journal Entry

Read this example of a journal entry.

Writing Model

August 27, 2012

Grandpa took me for a ride on the lake in his new motorboat today. The boat is red and white. It goes very fast! I thought the ride was great, but Grandpa didn't. The wind was strong and the waves were high. The boat kept dipping into the waves. Every time it popped back up, we got wet. Grandpa said the boat ride made him sick, but I enjoyed it. By the end of the day, all my clothes were dripping wet. I smelled like a fish, but I didn't mind!

Writer's Purpose: to record thoughts and feelings about a boat ride

© Evan-Moor Corp. • EMC 6012 • Nonfiction Writing   NARRATIVE WRITING   147

Name: _____

Journal Entry

Presenting the Topic

Read each question. Then write a topic sentence that answers the question.

Example
What did you do this week for the first time ever?
This week, I did a back flip for the first time.

1. What is the most exciting thing you did this week?
   This week, I went down the tallest and scariest slide at the water park.

2. What do you dream about doing when you grow up?
   I dream of driving a race car when I grow up.

3. What did you do this month that made you proud?
   I felt proud when I won the 100-yard dash at school last week.

4. What is the funniest thing you saw or heard this week?
   Yesterday, Mr. Sosa told us a funny joke at recess.

5. What is one thing you often wonder about?
   I wonder what makes stars twinkle.

148   NARRATIVE WRITING   Nonfiction Writing • EMC 6012 • © Evan-Moor Corp.

Lesson 1   Introducing a Journal Entry

A journal entry is a record of someone's personal thoughts and feelings about a topic or event.

1. Say: **In a journal, you write about things that have happened to you recently or that you wonder about. The writing you do each time is called an** *entry.*

2. Direct students to p. 147. Say: **Journal entries usually start with the date.** Ask: **What is the date of this journal entry?** (August 27) Read the entry aloud as students follow along. Tell students to focus on the writer's thoughts and feelings of that day's events.

3. Ask: **What is the purpose of this journal entry?** (to record thoughts and feelings about a boat ride) Have students write the purpose on the lines provided.

4. Invite students to offer opinions about what makes this a good journal entry. Prompt students by asking: **Do you know when the entry was written? Does the first sentence clearly tell what the entry is about? Does the writer share what he thinks and feels? Does he include good details about the topic? Are the events in an order that makes sense?**

5. Explain that students will use the model as they study the skills needed to write a good journal entry.

➤ **Extend the Lesson:** Explain to students that an online journal is called a *Web log,* or *blog* for short. Direct them to blogs that children frequently contribute to, and discuss different blog categories (e.g., books, music, sports, travel). Point out dates and reader responses if any are posted.

Lesson 2   Presenting the Topic

1. Explain that a journal entry tells about one event or one idea. Say: **The first sentence should tell what the journal entry is about.**

2. Refer to the model on p. 147 and ask: **What is this journal entry about?** (a ride in a new motorboat) Have a volunteer read the first sentence aloud. Ask: **Does this sentence tell what the entry is about?** (yes)

3. Direct students to p. 148 and read aloud the example. Ask: **Does the sentence answer the question "What did you do this week for the first time ever?"** (yes) **If this were the first sentence of a journal entry, what would the journal entry be about?** (doing a back flip)

4. Reread the example question aloud and ask: **How would you answer this question?** Invite two or three students to respond. Then read aloud the other questions. Remind students that a journal is a good place to write about things that have happened to them recently or things they wonder about. Have students complete the activity independently or in pairs. Invite volunteers to share their sentences.

➤ **Extend the Lesson:** Have students reread blog entries and check to see if the first sentence introduces the topic.

Lesson 3 Expressing Thoughts and Feelings

1. Say: **A journal is a good place to express your thoughts and feelings. You can tell how you feel about something or what you think about something that happens. The words you write should sound like you.**

2. Review the model on p. 147 and have students underline each sentence that expresses the writer's thoughts and feelings. (*I thought the ride was great …* and *I smelled like a fish, but I didn't mind!*)

3. Direct students to p. 149 and discuss the example. Then read aloud item 1, and model by saying: **I like Saturday mornings because I get to eat breakfast in bed.** Have students complete the activity in pairs or small groups. Invite volunteers to share their sentences with the class. Point out that even if some students feel the same way about a topic, they write about it in ways that make the writing personal.

➤ **Extend the Lesson:** Have students write two sentences that express their own thoughts and feelings about their last birthday.

Lesson 4 Giving Details in Order

1. Say: **When you write a journal entry about something that happened to you, give the details in the order that they happened. You can also tell how you felt about each part of the event.**

2. Reread the first two sentences of the model on p. 147. Then say: **The rest of the journal entry gives details about the boat ride in the order that they happened.** Ask: **What was the boat ride like?** (bumpy, wet) **How did the writer feel about it?** (He enjoyed it.) **Why didn't Grandpa enjoy it?** (The ride made him feel sick.) Point out that the writer told his thoughts and feelings between telling good details.

Page 149 / Student Book Page 109

Name: _____

Journal Entry

Expressing Thoughts and Feelings

Read each question. Write a sentence that explains how you think or feel.

Example
How do you feel at birthday parties?
I am happy because there is cake and ice cream.

1. What do Saturday mornings make you think about?
Saturday mornings make me think about having fun.

2. How do you feel just before bedtime?
I am sad because I want to stay up longer.

3. How do you feel when you do well on a test?
I feel proud of myself.

4. What does the color red remind you of?
Red reminds me of Valentine's Day.

5. How do you feel when your parents make your favorite dinner?
I feel special.

6. What do you think about at the end of the school day?
I think about going home to see my hamster.

© Evan-Moor Corp. • EMC 6012 • Nonfiction Writing   NARRATIVE WRITING 149

Page 150 / Student Book Page 110

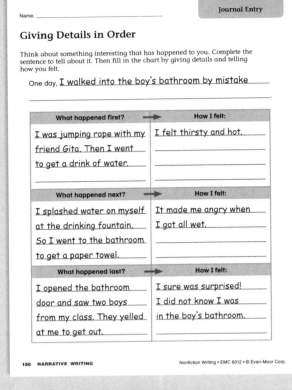

Page 151 and Sample Revision / Student Book Page 111

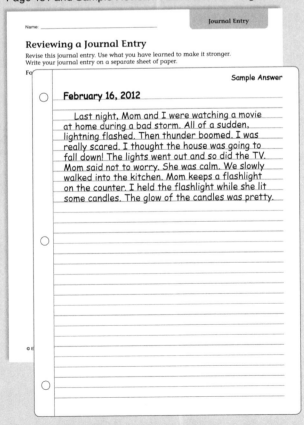

3. Direct students to p. 150 and read aloud the directions. Prompt students to name strange, funny, or scary things that have happened to them. List events on the board. (e.g., I went to the dentist. I saw a snake in my backyard. I dreamed that I went to school in my pajamas.) Demonstrate how to give details about an event by breaking it down into separate, sequential events. (e.g., I was walking down the sidewalk. Then I slipped on a banana peel and fell. As I was lying on the ground, some kid nearly stepped on me. It was a friend I had not seen since he changed schools last year.) Have students complete the activity in pairs or independently. Invite volunteers to share their stories with the class.

➤ **Extend the Lesson:** Have students add details for one of the sentences they wrote on p. 148.

Lesson 5 Reviewing a Journal Entry

1. Review the qualities of a good journal entry: a date, a topic sentence that introduces the event or idea, and details that include thoughts and feelings about the event or idea.

2. Read the journal entry on p. 151 as students follow along. Then guide students through revising the draft. Ask: **Did the writer include a date for the journal entry?** (no) Help students choose a suitable date for the entry. Then ask: **What event is the journal entry about?** (a storm) Ask: **Does the sentence "I was really scared" say what happened?** (no) Suggest that students move the first sentence so it comes *after* the detail that tells a scary thing that happened. Then reread this sentence: *The lights went out and so did the TV.* Ask: **Does the writer tell how she felt when the lights went out?** (no) Explain that this would be a good place to add a sentence that expresses thoughts or feelings. Then ask: **Do you know how the writer felt after her mom lit the candles?** (no) Point out that this would be another good place to add a sentence that focuses on thoughts or feelings.

3. Have students write their revised journal entries on a separate sheet of paper. Invite volunteers to share their revisions with the class.

Introducing a Journal Entry

Read this example of a journal entry.

Writing Model

August 27, 2012

Grandpa took me for a ride on the lake in his new motorboat today. The boat is red and white. It goes very fast! I thought the ride was great, but Grandpa didn't. The wind was strong and the waves were high. The boat kept dipping into the waves. Every time it popped back up, we got wet. Grandpa said the boat ride made him sick, but I enjoyed it. By the end of the day, all my clothes were dripping wet. I smelled like a fish, but I didn't mind!

Writer's Purpose: _____

_____

Presenting the Topic

Read each question. Then write a topic sentence that answers the question.

> **Example**
>
> What did you do this week for the first time ever?
>
> <u>This week, I did a back flip for the first time.</u>

1. What is the most exciting thing you did this week?

   _____

   _____

2. What do you dream about doing when you grow up?

   _____

   _____

3. What did you do this month that made you proud?

   _____

   _____

4. What is the funniest thing you saw or heard this week?

   _____

   _____

5. What is one thing you often wonder about?

   _____

   _____

Expressing Thoughts and Feelings

Read each question. Write a sentence that explains how you think or feel.

Example

How do you feel at birthday parties?

<u>I am happy because there is cake and ice cream.</u>

1. What do Saturday mornings make you think about?

_____

2. How do you feel just before bedtime?

_____

3. How do you feel when you do well on a test?

_____

4. What does the color red remind you of?

_____

5. How do you feel when your parents make your favorite dinner?

_____

6. What do you think about at the end of the school day?

_____

Giving Details in Order

Think about something interesting that has happened to you. Complete the sentence to tell about it. Then fill in the chart by giving details and telling how you felt.

One day, _____

_____.

What happened first? ➡	**How I felt:**
_____	_____
_____	_____
_____	_____
_____	_____

What happened next? ➡	**How I felt:**
_____	_____
_____	_____
_____	_____
_____	_____

What happened last? ➡	**How I felt:**
_____	_____
_____	_____
_____	_____
_____	_____

Reviewing a Journal Entry

Revise this journal entry. Use what you have learned to make it stronger.
Write your journal entry on a separate sheet of paper.

Focus on:

✓ starting with the date
✓ telling what the journal entry is about
✓ giving details about the events in the order they happened
✓ telling what you thought or felt about the events

Draft

I was really scared. Mom and I were
watching a movie. We slowly walked into the
kitchen. All of a sudden, lightning flashed.
Then thunder boomed. The lights went out
and so did the TV. Mom keeps a flashlight
on the counter. I held the flashlight while
she lit some candles.

Writing Creative Nonfiction

Page 155 / Student Book Page 113

Name: _____

Creative Nonfiction

Introducing Creative Nonfiction
Read this example of creative nonfiction.

Writing Model

Kit, the Happy Otter

It was an exciting day at the Monterey Bay Aquarium otter tank. Visitors watched two sea otters named Kit and Mae swim in the big tank. Kit, the baby otter, had gotten lost on the beach when she was very young. Now the older otter, Mae, was teaching Kit what otters should know. Mae swam across the tank. Kit zigzagged after her as fast as lightning. A worker tossed a handful of smelly clams into the water. Splash! Mae grabbed a clam. Then Kit grabbed a clam, too. She rolled onto her back and stuffed the juicy clam into her mouth. Kit was happy in her new home.

Writer's Purpose: _to tell a true story about a baby otter_
_____

© Evan-Moor Corp. • EMC 6012 • Nonfiction Writing   **NARRATIVE WRITING 155**

Lesson 1 Introducing Creative Nonfiction

Creative nonfiction is writing that tells a true story in an interesting way.

1. Suggest a nonfiction topic such as the first Thanksgiving. Say: **A nonfiction book about the first Thanksgiving could just give facts. But a *creative* nonfiction book would give the facts about the first Thanksgiving by telling a story.** Explain that writers of creative nonfiction tell about things that really happened, but reading their text is like reading a story.

2. Read aloud "Kit, the Happy Otter" on p. 155 as students follow along.

3. Ask: **What is the purpose of this piece of creative nonfiction?** (to tell a true story about a baby otter) Have students write the purpose on the lines provided.

4. Invite students to offer opinions about what makes this good creative nonfiction. Prompt students by asking: **Does the first sentence tell what the paragraph is about? Does it make you want to read on? Does the writer tell a true story? Does she use clear details that help you picture what you're reading?**

5. Explain that students will use the model as they study the skills needed to write creative nonfiction.

➤ **Extend the Lesson:** Read other examples of creative nonfiction to the class, and have students identify the facts in each true story.

Lesson 2 Writing a Creative First Sentence

1. Review the purpose of creative nonfiction. (to tell a true story in a creative way) Then say: **In creative nonfiction, the writer begins with a sentence that sparks the reader's imagination. It should also hint at what the story is about.**

2. Write these two sentences on the board: *It was an exciting day at the Monterey Bay Aquarium otter tank. The Monterey Bay Aquarium has an otter tank.* Ask: **Which of these sentences sounds like the beginning of a story?** (the first one) Invite volunteers to describe the mental images that the first sentence evokes. (e.g., a crowd of people, blue water, brown otters, splashing sounds) Say: **A good first sentence for creative nonfiction should sound as if it comes from a storybook and should get readers interested in the topic.**

3. Read aloud the directions for Activity A on p. 156. Then read the first pair of sentences. Ask: **Which sentence is more interesting and uses words that help you form a clear picture in your mind?** Have students complete the activity in pairs. Review the answers and ask students to explain their choices.

4. Read the directions for Activity B and ask a volunteer to read the first paragraph. Ask: **How can we change the first sentence to make it more interesting? What details could we use that tell where the bee is and what it is doing?** Then have students suggest possible rewrites. Record their suggestions on the board and guide them to identify the best choice. Then have students complete the activity independently.

➤ **Extend the Lesson:** Suggest a few nonfiction topics (e.g., animals that hibernate, desert plants). Have partners choose a topic and write an interesting first sentence for a piece of creative nonfiction on that topic.

Lesson 3 Using Sensory Details

1. Say: **Using details that describe how something looks, sounds, feels, smells, or tastes helps readers imagine the ideas in the text.** Have students name things that they could describe using sensory details. (e.g., salty chips, smelly garbage, soft bunnies)

2. Review the model on p. 155 and have students look for sensory details. (e.g., sight: *Kit zigzagged;* smell: *tossed a handful of smelly clams;* sound: *Splash!* taste: *stuffed the juicy clam into her mouth*)

3. Read aloud the directions for Activity A on p. 157. To activate prior knowledge, invite volunteers to describe their experiences with outdoor activities at night, such as camping or watching fireworks. Encourage them to tell what they heard, what the night air felt like or smelled like, and what they saw in the sky. Then conduct the activity with the class.

4. Read aloud the directions for Activity B. Then read the paragraph as students follow along. Have students complete the activity independently, drawing on the sensory details they brainstormed in Activity A.

➤ **Extend the Lesson:** Have students write a description of their favorite food without naming it. Then have them exchange descriptions with a partner and try to guess the favorite food.

Page 156 / Student Book Page 114

Name: _____   Creative Nonfiction

Writing a Creative First Sentence

A. Read each pair of sentences. Choose the sentence that is more interesting and that sounds more like the beginning of a story.

1. ☑ A robot named Spirit had been wandering on Mars for many years.
   ☐ Scientists sent a robot to Mars.

2. ☐ Some parrots can talk.
   ☑ Alex was a special parrot that could talk, count, and choose colors.

3. ☐ A lot of people like to visit the Grand Canyon, which is in Arizona.
   ☑ The Grand Canyon has colorful rocks and blue skies.

4. ☑ An ape named Suryia and his dog Roscoe take a walk.
   ☐ There is an ape who likes to take walks with a dog.

B. Read each paragraph. Rewrite the first sentence to make it more creative.

1. A honeybee flies around. She lands on a purple flower and gathers nectar. She carries the sticky nectar to her hive. She gives the nectar to another worker bee. Then she flies away again to search for more flowers.

A honeybee buzzes around pretty flowers.
_____

2. The scientist worked. She dug in the ground with a sharp tool. The dirt was warm and brown. The day was hot. The scientist stopped to take a drink of water. Then she noticed a strange rock. It was a dinosaur bone!

The scientist hunted for dinosaur bones.
_____

156 NARRATIVE WRITING   Nonfiction Writing • EMC 6012 • © Evan-Moor Corp.

Page 157 / Student Book Page 115

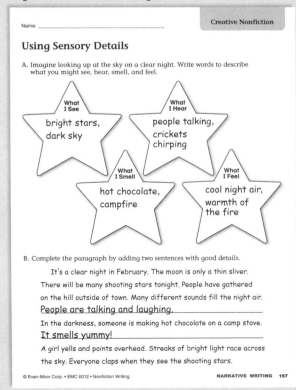

Name: _____   Creative Nonfiction

Using Sensory Details

A. Imagine looking up at the sky on a clear night. Write words to describe what you might see, hear, smell, and feel.

What I See: bright stars, dark sky

What I Hear: people talking, crickets chirping

What I Smell: hot chocolate, campfire

What I Feel: cool night air, warmth of the fire

B. Complete the paragraph by adding two sentences with good details.

It's a clear night in February. The moon is only a thin sliver. There will be many shooting stars tonight. People have gathered on the hill outside of town. Many different sounds fill the night air. People are talking and laughing. In the darkness, someone is making hot chocolate on a camp stove. It smells yummy! A girl yells and points overhead. Streaks of bright light race across the sky. Everyone claps when they see the shooting stars.

© Evan-Moor Corp. • EMC 6012 • Nonfiction Writing   **NARRATIVE WRITING** **157**

Writing Creative Nonfiction, continued

Using Similes

A. Complete each simile about the Fourth of July by choosing from the box.

| a cloud | an iceberg | bird wings | jewels | snakes | thunder |

1. The drums in the parade are as loud as ___thunder___.
2. American flags flap like ___bird wings___.
3. The watermelon is as cold as ___an iceberg___.
4. The pink cotton candy is as fluffy as ___a cloud___.
5. Hot dogs cooking on the grill hiss like ___snakes___.
6. Fireworks sparkle in the sky like ___jewels___.

B. Write a word or phrase to complete each simile.

1. The moon is as round as ___a tortilla___
2. The night sky is as dark as ___mud___
3. The sun is like ___a huge yellow ball___
4. The sunset is like ___streaks of orange paint___
5. The stars are like ___white sprinkles on chocolate cupcakes___

158 NARRATIVE WRITING   Nonfiction Writing • EMC 6012 • © Evan-Moor Corp.

Page 159 and Sample Revision / Student Book Page 117

Reviewing Creative Nonfiction

Revise this example of creative nonfiction. Use what you have learned to make it stronger. Write it on a separate sheet of paper.

Sample Answer

A Tasty Mistake

Ruth Wakefield's kitchen always smelled like fresh-baked cookies. She baked cookies every day for her guests at the Toll House Inn. One day, Ruth wanted to make chocolate cookies. But the box of powdered chocolate was empty. All she had was a chocolate bar. So she broke it into tiny pieces and stirred the pieces into the cookie dough. Ruth hoped that the chocolate would melt completely and mix into the creamy batter. Instead, it stayed as chocolate bits. The cookies looked like freckled faces. They were sweet and delicious. Ruth had created chocolate chip cookies by mistake.

Lesson 4 Using Similes

1. Say: **A simile is a comparison that uses the word** *like* **or** *as*. **Writers use similes to describe things in a creative way.** Display an object, such as a ruler, and describe it using a simile. (e.g., This ruler is as straight as an arrow.) Then ask: **What two things am I comparing?** (e.g., a ruler and an arrow) **How are they similar?** (Both are straight.) Prompt students to use other similes to describe the object. (e.g., as light as a feather, shiny like glass)

2. Have students identify the simile in "Kit, the Happy Otter." *(as fast as lightning)* Ask: **What two things does this simile compare?** (lightning and how fast Kit swims) **How are these things alike?** (Both are fast.)

3. Read aloud the directions for Activity A on p. 158. Explain: **These sentences describe things you might experience at a Fourth of July celebration.** Model completing the first simile. Say: **This simile compares drums to something else that is loud. Thunder is also loud, so I'll choose that word.** Have students complete the activity independently.

4. Have students complete Activity B in small groups. Then invite groups to share their similes with the class.

➤ **Extend the Lesson:** Invite students to write two similes about themselves, based on physical attributes or personality traits.

Lesson 5 Reviewing Creative Nonfiction

1. Review the qualities of good creative nonfiction: a creative first sentence, sensory details, and descriptive language that includes similes.

2. Direct students to p. 159. Explain that this paragraph tells the true story of an innkeeper who invented a kind of cookie. Read the passage aloud to students. Then guide them through the revision. Say: **Let's improve the first sentence.** Ask: **How can we make the detail stronger?** (e.g., replace *good* with *sweet* or *buttery*) Prompt students to offer details that describe Ruth's reaction when she realized there was no powdered chocolate. Then ask: **What detail could we add that will help readers picture Ruth mixing the cookie dough?** (e.g., tell how the dough smelled or what it looked like) **What do chocolate chips look like in baked cookies?** (e.g., big freckles, polka dots)

3. Have students write their revisions on a separate sheet of paper. Invite volunteers to read their revisions aloud.

Name: _____

Introducing Creative Nonfiction

Read this example of creative nonfiction.

Kit, the Happy Otter

It was an exciting day at the Monterey Bay Aquarium otter tank. Visitors watched two sea otters named Kit and Mae swim in the big tank. Kit, the baby otter, had gotten lost on the beach when she was very young. Now the older otter, Mae, was teaching Kit what otters should know. Mae swam across the tank. Kit zigzagged after her as fast as lightning. A worker tossed a handful of smelly clams into the water. Splash! Mae grabbed a clam. Then Kit grabbed a clam, too. She rolled onto her back and stuffed the juicy clam into her mouth. Kit was happy in her new home.

Writer's Purpose: _____

_____

Writing a Creative First Sentence

A. Read each pair of sentences. Choose the sentence that is more interesting and that sounds more like the beginning of a story.

1. ☐ A robot named Spirit had been wandering on Mars for many years.
   ☐ Scientists sent a robot to Mars.

2. ☐ Some parrots can talk.
   ☐ Alex was a special parrot that could talk, count, and choose colors.

3. ☐ A lot of people like to visit the Grand Canyon, which is in Arizona.
   ☐ The Grand Canyon has colorful rocks and blue skies.

4. ☐ An ape named Suryia and his dog Roscoe take a walk.
   ☐ There is an ape who likes to take walks with a dog.

B. Read each paragraph. Rewrite the first sentence to make it more creative.

1. <u>A honeybee flies around.</u> She lands on a purple flower and gathers nectar. She carries the sticky nectar to her hive. She gives the nectar to another worker bee. Then she flies away again to search for more flowers.

   _____

   _____

2. <u>The scientist worked.</u> She dug in the ground with a sharp tool. The dirt was warm and brown. The day was hot. The scientist stopped to take a drink of water. Then she noticed a strange rock. It was a dinosaur bone!

   _____

   _____

Using Sensory Details

A. Imagine looking up at the sky on a clear night. Write words to describe what you might see, hear, smell, and feel.

What I See

What I Hear

What I Smell

What I Feel

B. Complete the paragraph by adding two sentences with good details.

It's a clear night in February. The moon is only a thin sliver. There will be many shooting stars tonight. People have gathered on the hill outside of town. Many different sounds fill the night air.

_____

In the darkness, someone is making hot chocolate on a camp stove.

_____

A girl yells and points overhead. Streaks of bright light race across the sky. Everyone claps when they see the shooting stars.

Using Similes

A. Complete each simile about the Fourth of July by choosing from the box.

a cloud	**an iceberg**	**bird wings**	**jewels**	**snakes**	**thunder**

1. The drums in the parade are as loud as _____.

2. American flags flap like _____.

3. The watermelon is as cold as _____.

4. The pink cotton candy is as fluffy as _____.

5. Hot dogs cooking on the grill hiss like _____.

6. Fireworks sparkle in the sky like _____.

B. Write a word or phrase to complete each simile.

1. The moon is as round as _____.

2. The night sky is as dark as _____.

3. The sun is like _____.

4. The sunset is like _____.

5. The stars are like _____.

Name: _____

Reviewing Creative Nonfiction

Revise this example of creative nonfiction. Use what you have learned to make it stronger. Write it on a separate sheet of paper.

Focus on:
- ✓ writing a creative first sentence
- ✓ telling how something sounds, feels, looks, smells, or tastes
- ✓ using similes to describe things

Draft

A Tasty Mistake

Ruth Wakefield's kitchen always smelled good. She baked cookies every day for her guests at the Toll House Inn. One day, Ruth wanted to make chocolate cookies. But the box of powdered chocolate was empty. All she had was a chocolate bar. So she broke it up and stirred it into the cookie dough. Ruth hoped that the chocolate would melt and mix into the batter. Instead, it stayed as chocolate bits. Ruth had created chocolate chip cookies by mistake.

Skill Sharpeners Spell & Write

AWARD-WINNING*

Grades PreK–6+ • *Skill Sharpeners* provides at-home practice that helps students master and retain skills. Each book in this dynamic series is the ideal resource for programs such as summer school, after school, remediation, and school book fairs & fundraising. 144 full-color pages.

- *activities aligned with national and state standards*
- *assessment pages in standardized-test format*
- *full color, charmingly illustrated, and kid-friendly*

Spell & Write

PreK	EMC 4535-PRO	3	EMC 4539-PRO
K	EMC 4536-PRO	4	EMC 4540-PRO
1	EMC 4537-PRO	5	EMC 4541-PRO
2	EMC 4538-PRO	6+	EMC 4542-PRO

*The National Parenting Center, Seal of Approval Winner
*iParenting Media Awards Outstanding Product

Grade 3
Spell & Write

Daily Paragraph Editing Interactive Application

Grades 2–6+ • Present your students with engaging and interactive editing practice. The *Daily Paragraph Editing* interactive app helps students practice critical mechanics and usage skills while they click and drag editing marks into place, type in corrections, and check their work with the click of a button. Use the lessons with your interactive whiteboard, personal computer, or projection system to motivate learning and enrich instruction.

	Class Pack*		Single Classroom License		Annual Maintenance Subscription
2	EMC 9712-PRO	2	EMC 5622-PRO	2	EMC 5682-PRO
3	EMC 9713-PRO	3	EMC 5623-PRO	3	EMC 5683-PRO
4	EMC 9714-PRO	4	EMC 5624-PRO	4	EMC 5684-PRO
5	EMC 9715-PRO	5	EMC 5625-PRO	5	EMC 5685-PRO
6+	EMC 9716-PRO	6+	EMC 5626-PRO	6+	EMC 5686-PRO

Daily Language Review Interactive Application

Grades 1–8 • Engage students in interactive language practice using 180 dynamic lessons. The *Daily Language Review* interactive app covers grammar, punctuation, usage, and sentence-editing skills while encouraging collaborative learning and participation. Use the lessons with your interactive whiteboard, personal computer, or projection system to motivate learning and enrich instruction.

	Class Pack*		Single Classroom License		Annual Maintenance Subscription
1	EMC 9721-PRO	1	EMC 5641-PRO	1	EMC 5691-PRO
2	EMC 9722-PRO	2	EMC 5642-PRO	2	EMC 5692-PRO
3	EMC 9723-PRO	3	EMC 5643-PRO	3	EMC 5693-PRO
4	EMC 9724-PRO	4	EMC 5644-PRO	4	EMC 5694-PRO
5	EMC 9725-PRO	5	EMC 5645-PRO	5	EMC 5695-PRO
6	EMC 9726-PRO	6	EMC 5646-PRO	6	EMC 5696-PRO
7	EMC 9727-PRO	7	EMC 5647-PRO	7	EMC 5697-PRO
8	EMC 9728-PRO	8	EMC 5648-PRO	8	EMC 5698-PRO

* Class Pack includes: Interactive Application, Teacher's Edition, 20 Student Books